THE
KINSHIP WARS

An Essay on the Prehistory of
Social Anthropology

William Y. Adams

ARCHWAY
PUBLISHING

Archway Publishing books may be ordered through booksellers or by contacting:

Archway Publishing
1663 Liberty Drive
Bloomington, IN 47403
www.archwaypublishing.com
1 (888) 242-5904

ISBN: 978-1-4808-5487-1 (sc)
ISBN: 978-1-4808-5485-7 (hc)
ISBN: 978-1-4808-5486-4 (e)

Library of Congress Control Number: 2018900006

Print information available on the last page.

Archway Publishing rev. date: 01/16/2018

CONTENTS

CHAPTER ONE

BACKGROUND FACTORS

The discipline of social anthropology was born in the later nineteenth century, when four men in four different countries more or less simultaneously "discovered" kinship. That is, they noticed that both blood relationships and marital relationships were computed in very different ways by different peoples and in different ages. Earlier social thinkers, though sensitive to varieties of social organization, had taken "the family" of one husband, one wife, and their children as a given at all times and places, assuming it to be a law of nature. The "discoverers" noticed for the first time that there were different kinds and numbers of husbands, different kinds and numbers of wives, and a truly extraordinary variety of aunts, uncles, cousins, and grandparents, involving different expectations and obligations.

The legal context

It would be hard to imagine a more disparate group of men than the four "discoverers," none of whom knew each other at the time. They were the mystically romantic Swiss Johann Bachofen, the serenely detached English Henry Sumner Maine, the ever-contentious Scot John McLennan, and the American man of affairs Lewis Henry Morgan. They had however one thing in common: they had all been trained in the law. So also had three of the later theorists discussed in these pages: Staniland Wake, Josef Kohler, and Edwin Hartland.

1

Their earliest and most important "discoveries" were matrilineal descent, corporate kin groups, exogamy, and the enormous diversity of systems of nomenclature. Those discoveries did not derive from the study of comparative ethnography, which hardly existed in their day. If anything, it was the other way around; early ethnography was inspired to a considerable extent, and its research direction set, by the discovery of variable kinship. The jurists were inspired rather by the study of law itself, and more particularly its history. All of them except Wake were professors rather than practicing barristers, and they were led to the contemplation of primitive society in their attempt to find the original sources of law. They found, among the institutions of primitive society, that the one most nearly comparable to today's codified law is the kinship system. It is highly formal, at least some of its requirements are clearly spelled out, it applies to everyone without exception, it is known to everyone, and it relates to the relations between persons. Also and importantly, it usually regulates the ownership and transfer of property—among the most fundamental concerns of Western, Roman-derived law. To the extent that it laid absolute obligations and restrictions on everyone, kinship *was* law.

The evolutionary dimension

In the later nineteenth century, Evolution was the watchword of the age, thanks almost entirely to Charles Darwin. However, many intellectuals carried the idea far beyond anything imagined by Darwin. Liberated from scriptural dogma, evolution for them took the place of God as the explanation of just about everything in both nature and history. Often it was just another name for Progress--the backbone of western historical thinking for two thousand years and more--but the new name gave it for the first time the cachet of Science rather than mere optimism.

Early Greek philosophers had long ago devised what today we would call social evolutionary scenarios, even involving successive stages based on modes of subsistence. After a millennium in abeyance, this idea was revived and very much further elaborated by thinkers of the French and Scottish Enlightenments. They conceived either of three stages—hunting, pastoralism, and agriculture--or four stages, with civilization added as a triumphal culmination. In Scotland, Adam Ferguson even coined the terms Savagery, Barbarism, and Civilization, made famous a century later by Lewis Henry Morgan, to whom they are usually attributed. (For extended discussion see Adams 1998, 22-31).

Lacking any semblance of archaeological evidence, the Enlightenment scholars formed their views of the earliest human societies and cultures mainly through the "logic of subtraction," or turning progress on its head. Whatever was complex in the world of today must have been simple in the beginning, and the more complex today, the simpler at the beginning. The earliest humans had only the rudiments of society, the rudiments of religion, and even the simplest of languages, they believed. From that starting point, social and cultural evolution was largely a matter of increasing complexity.

The early philosophers also lacked any notion of the true antiquity of man. Though by no means scriptural fundamentalists, they tended to accept the very short chronology of human existence that Biblical scholars had worked out, based on their computation of the genealogies in the Old Testament. "This poor world, they tell us, is but six thousand years old," says Rosalind in the third act of Shakespeare's *As You Like It*.[1] Seen in that respect, the prehistoric scenarios of the philosophers were hardly more than an intellectual parlor game, applying as they did only to the very brief span of human existence preceding the earliest written records. No one considered them very important for our understanding of ourselves, until archeology unexpectedly stepped in.

Archaeology steps in

In the middle years of the nineteenth century, pioneer archaeologists turned the tables, with what was surely the most revolutionary discovery of its day. Almost simultaneously in France and in England, they found evidence that humans had existed in the far distant past, contemporary with long-extinct giant animals. Although it was to be more than a century before the enormous span of human prehistory was fully calculated,

---

[1] Note that this chronological reckoning has no actual basis in scripture.

it was from the beginning recognized to be far longer than the span of written history (see especially Daniel 1950, 57-62). More than just a parlor game for social philosophers, their evolutionary scenarios were now seen as our only key to understanding the longest part of our existence. Though no more founded on empirical evidence than before, they were now co-opted as genuine science. Borrowing the cachet of Darwin's work, they became part of the grand scheme of evolution.

In the climate of the times, when evolution in one form or another was "the rage of the age," it was inevitable that the discoverers of kinship should feel that their discoveries must fit somewhere within the evolutionary schema. More than just fitting in, they were seen by most of the armchair scholars as forming the basic foundation of the earliest human society. It was a generation and more before ethnographers were able so show that there was a lot more to primitive society than kinship.

Ethnography steps in

Until the end of the nineteenth century, Anglo-American theorists continued to base their evolutionary schemes mainly on logic, continuing the tradition of Enlightenment rationalism. Not so the Germanic scholars, whose main intellectual inspiration came not from Enlightenment rationalism but from the anti-Enlightenment philosophy of Immanuel Kant, with its mantra of *das Ding an sich* (the thing in itself). In the Kantian view everyone and everything has its own *Geist* or spirit or essence, the outcome of its individual heredity and history; it cannot be understood with reference to anything else. Put in the simplest terms, it could be said that the Anglo-Americans were interested in the similarities between peoples, and the Germans in the differences.

The Anglo-American and the Germanic proto-anthropologists shared in common a primary interest in reconstructing the long prehistory of human society. But while the Anglo-Americans continued to rely on logic, the Germanics[2] looked for enlightenment to the study of

---

[2] I have to use this awkward term because Bachofen, Starcke, Westermarck, and Lowie were not Germans in the strict sense; they were respectively Swiss, Danish, Swedish, and Austrian.

the most primitive peoples identifiable in their own time. The idea was certainly not a new one; as far back as 1690 John Locke had asserted that "In the beginning all the World was America" [referring specifically to North American Indians], and *"America . . . is still a pattern of the first Ages in Asia and Europe"* [italics in the original] (Locke 1690, 161; 383). A little later the missionary Joseph Lafitau had pursued the analogy much further with his *Customs of American Savages Compared with the Customs of Primitive Times* (Lafitau 1974; French original 1724). However it was the Germanics, in the latter half of the nineteenth century, who went actively in search of confirmation. Quite simply, they invented ethnography (including the term) as an active branch of natural history, along with zoology, botany, and geology. Before the end of the century there were local ethnographic or ethnological museums and societies in a number of German, Austrian, and Swiss cities. German ethnographers were active especially in Africa and South America. Just as importantly, the Germans as early as 1870 had begun to publish massive, multi-volume ethnographic encyclopedias, setting forth whatever was known about tribal societies and cultures all around the world. The Anglo-American theorists were not wholly deaf to ethnographic evidence; they were quick to cite it whenever it provided support for their theories. Their use of it however was always highly selective.

The difference between the two schools of thought is very evident in the case of the kinship wars. It was the Anglo-Americans who formulated grand, simplistic themes, while the Germanics (with the exception of Bachofen) continually pointed out that things were not that simple.

The wars

Matrilineal descent, corporate kin groups, widespread exogamy, and ramified systems of nomenclature were not found among modern civilized nations; Anglo Americans and Germans could agree that they must therefore represent earlier stages of evolutionary development. But just where did they fit? On that subject the kinship theorists disagreed, and their disputes became so heated that I have called them the "kinship wars." That heat seems ludicrous today, but in its time a proper understanding of evolutionary stages, encompassing systems of kinship, was regarded as essential to our proper understanding of ourselves. My purpose then is to consider, each in his turn, the "discoverers" of kinship and their ideas, right and wrong. There were plenty of both. I have omitted from discussion such luminaries as Sir James Frazer and Sir John Lubbock, who wrote extensively on kinship but had nothing original to say about it.

CHAPTER TWO

JOHANN BACHOFEN AND MATRILINEAL INHERITANCE

Johann Jacob Bachofen (1815-1887) was the scion of an old, prominent, and very wealthy family in the city of Basel, Switzerland. Many of his ancestors had been municipal counselors and burgomasters. Young Johann's circumstances were such that he never really had to support himself, and in later life he made no pretense to doing so. He devoted his life to his own education.

Bachofen went to university because it was always expected of the Germanic *haute bourgeoisie,* and chose Law because he had to do something with himself. From earliest youth however he had strong antiquarian proclivities, and he was always much more interested in the history of law than in its practice. His studies took him in time to the University of Berlin and to the classroom of Friedrich von Savigny, one of the outstanding juristic philosophers of the time and the author of a book on *The Law of Property.* He was an exponent of the view that the law is a mirror of its times, and its earliest inspiration can be found in ancient mythology. In an unpublished essay, "My Life in Retrospect," (Bachofen 1967, 3-17) Bachofen named a truly prodigious number of intellectual influences, but von Savigny was undoubtedly the most important among them.

In his search for enlightenment Bachofen spent periods in London, in Paris, and in Rome. In these places he was not pursuing formal studies, but merely seeking like a good ethnographer for an understanding of the societies around him. Returned to Basel, his family status led to his appointment as a member of the Grand Council of the Basel criminal court, and a little later as its vice-president. In due time he was also given honorary offices as Professor of Roman Law, Curator of the University, and Judge of the Court of Appeal. But after a late and apparently advantageous marriage he turned his back entirely on the world of affairs, and devoted the remainder of his life to scholarship. He died of a stroke at the age of 72.

Like his mentor von Savigny, Bachofen's studies of law led him into mythology, which had in fact been one of his earliest interests. He felt like Savigny that mythology held the key to the earliest forms of society, and the sources of law. To him the fantastic content of the ancient myths was irrelevant; what was important was that they offered a mirror on the mind-set of their tellers and listeners, and the society of their times, as well as on the origins of later institutions.

Secluded from the world of reality in his ivory tower, Bachofen in later life devoted himself entirely to the study of mythology and of ancient art. He was above all interested in their symbolic content, which held worlds of meaning for those who knew how to interpret it. "Myth is the exegesis of the symbol," he wrote (Bachofen 1967, 48). Over time his ideas on the subject became more and more fanciful and mystical, and invited a certain amount of ridicule from other scholars. His earliest book *An Essay on Mortuary Symbolism* (translated title), published in 1859, exhibits to the full his penchant for far-fetched imagination. Three eggs, resting on a table in an Etruscan tomb painting, clearly represented the force of life and reproduction (Bachofen 1967, 24-30); a flickering lamp captures the soul of Psyche, while its hot oil is "striving for union with Eros" (Bachofen 1967, 47). In Bachofen's view these interpretations are evident to any thinking person.

Das Mutterrecht

Bachofen's major discovery that concerns us here, that of matrilineal inheritance, was the entire subject of his second book, *The Mother-Right*

(Das Mutterrecht), published in 1861. The idea was suggested to him by his studies both of mythology and of law. It was not absolutely original with him; a hundred years earlier matrilineal inheritance had already been noted in passing by the Scottish social philosophers Adam Ferguson and John Millar (see Adams 1996, 26-7). However, neither of them attached any great importance to it, while Bachofen saw in it the foundation for the earliest human society.

The explanation in Bachofen's mind was simple and obvious. His vision of he earliest human society, shared with a good many early evolutionary thinkers, was of a leader-less, promiscuous horde, something like a troop of baboons. (He did not of course use that analogy; the connection between humans and apes had yet to be made.) There was no such thing as marriage; matings were essentially "one-night stands." Consequently, when children were born, there was no certainty as to the paternity. The bond of mother to child was the one social bond that existed in the earliest society. "At the lowest, darkest stages of human existence the love between the mother and her offspring is the bright spot in life, the only light in the moral darkness . . ." (Bachofen 1967, 79). All other social bonds sprang from it.

Das Mutterrecht begins, like all Bachofen's books, with a lengthy Introduction in which he sets out his thinking in very general terms, and identifies his sources. This is followed by shorter chapters in which he discusses the evidence for matriliny-matriarchy in Lycia (his starting point), Athens, Lemnos, Egypt, India, and Lesbos.

Bachofen never explored the more extended aspects of matrilineal kinship as we understand them today, for he had little recourse to ethnographic data. Unilineal systems of nomenclature, lineages, and exogamy were alike beyond his ken, hence aunts, uncles, and cousins played no part in his scheme. Instead, his thought branched out in another direction: he saw in matrilineal descent the genesis of matriarchy, the earliest form of human government. "Starting from Herodotus' account of the Lycians as matrilineal, Bachofen deduces from it a coherent system of law antecedent and antithetical to the patriarchal principle of antiquity. Not only did children take their mother's name in Lycia, but women ruled the household as well as the state" (Lowie 1937, 41-2). Women gained their political ascendency through their "aptitude for religion" (Bachofen 1967, 91). Thus, for Bachofen, "Mother-right" embraced both matriliny and matriarchy. Matriliny existed from the beginning of society, while matriarchy emerged with the coming of agriculture. Throughout his work the author discourses on the "beauty" and the moral superiority of the two systems, expressing essentially the superior virtue of the female.

Bachofen published one more book, *The Myth of Tanaquil,* in 1870. It was a kind of logical sequel to *Mutterrecht,* for in it he traced the gradual emergence of male supremacy, as revealed in a long series of ancient myths, culminating in the final triumph of Rome. ". . . It was a victory gained only at the cost of a ruthless suppression and subordination of the claims and allures of the natural world . . ." (Bachofen 1967, xlviii).

Perspective

Bachofen's one enduring contribution, for which he is deservedly remembered, was that of inserting matrilineal inheritance firmly into the evolutionary discourse, where it remains to this day. However, its proper place within that schema remains problematical. No one today except a few radical feminists believes that it was the original form of social organization. Ethnographic studies have shown that in the simplest societies known today descent is either patrilineal or bilateral (cf. Steward 1936). But matrilineal kinship is also not found in any of the world's more complex societies. In some sense therefore it must be reckoned as an evolutionary stage, falling somewhere between the earliest and the latest. Equally clear however is the fact that it was never universal.

The closest thing to a correlation with matriliny seems to be represented by swidden (hoe) agriculture, which was indeed a widespread and a critically important evolutionary development. The association however is by no means universal. Matriliny is found among at least some pre-agricultural or non-agricultural peoples, while there are plenty of swidden farmers who practice patrilineal descent. Both kinds of reckoning are found today among native Australians as well as different Pueblo Indian groups in the Southwest. At best, then, matrilineal organization must be seen as a possible alternative at certain stages of evolutionary development.

It remains only to add that Bachofen's idea of primeval matriarchy never caught on.

CHAPTER THREE

HENRY SUMNER MAINE AND THE CORPORATE KIN GROUP

Henry Sumner Maine (1822-1888), the son of a physician, was born near London[3] but spent most of his earliest youth on the island of Jersey, in the English Channel. In time however his parents separated and young Henry returned with his mother to England, settling at Reading, where his material grandparents lived. For the remainder of his youth Maine was brought up entirely by his mother, a well-educated woman from a genteel family.

In due course an influential godfather, the Bishop of Chester, got him a place in one of England's elite prep schools, from whence he went on to Pembroke College, Cambridge. As an undergraduate he achieved notice as a classical scholar, and also received a gold medal for poetry, which he wrote in both English and Latin. He graduated as a Senior Chancellor's Medalist in Classics in 1844. Shortly afterward he was appointed a tutor in one of the Cambridge colleges, and then as Regius (i.e. royally-endowed) Professor of Civil Law. He was admitted to the bar (i.e. to practice in court) in 1847 and also became a lecturer at the Inns of Court in London, England's most exclusive legal institution.

A turning point in Maine's life came in 1863 when he was appointed as legal member of the Governing Council of India, and spent the next

---

[3] Winters (1991, 436) errs in identifying his birthplace as Kelso, Scotland; this was his father's birthplace.

six years in that country. He dealt with a wide variety of issues, political, legal, and religious, and played a considerable part in shaping the codification of Indian civil law. His services were sufficiently appreciated so that he was asked to stay on for two years beyond his appointed four-year term, and on his return to England was rewarded with a knighthood.

In India Maine was obliged to steep himself deeply in Indian traditional law, and found it to be markedly different from the Roman-derived law of European countries. It was undoubtedly from that experience that he gained the cross-cultural perspective so evident in his later writing—a quality that set him apart from nearly all the other evolutionary thinkers of the time.

Returned to England in 1869, Maine was appointed Professor of Law at Oxford, but resigned the position five years later to become Master of Trinity Hall at Cambridge, where he had formerly been a tutor. Eventually he was also appointed Professor of International Law at Cambridge. He thus had the rare distinction of serving as a senior professor at both of England's elite universities. Neither position carried onerous teaching duties, allowing Maine to spend most of his time in later years in writing the books and articles for which he became famous.

Maine was much respected and honored during his lifetime, in contrast to the ridicule suffered by Bachofen. His books were admired and very widely read in many countries, and some remain in print today. This perhaps accounts for the tone of calm self-confidence evident in his writing—very different from the romantic effusion of Bachofen or the bumptious argumentation of John McLennan (see next chapter).

Maine was never a robust person, and his health gave way in 1887. He went off to the south of France under doctor's advice, but died there in the following year, at the age of 65. (More extended details of his life will be found in Grant Duff, 1892).

Ancient Law

Maine was first and last a teacher, and all four of his published books began originally as lecture series. *Ancient Law,* his first (1861), was based on a series of lectures delivered at Cambridge in the years prior to his departure for India (Pollock 1920, xviii). Those lectures were delivered to law students, and the phraseology and vocabulary of *Ancient Law* suggest at several points that the author still had the legal community primarily in mind. "In *Ancient Law* the reader constantly faces the unfamiliar problems of traditional jurisprudence. The very terminology is forbidding, the facts lie beyond his scope" as Lowie (1937, 50) put it. It may have surprised the author himself that the work reached a vastly wider audience. His main concern was the history of law rather than social evolution more broadly, but it was clearly the latter aspect, with its broad theoretical implications, which caused the book to "take off." It inserted itself squarely into what was the most exciting discourse of the times, and it went into multiple editions within a generation.

The scope of the work is set forth in its rarely-quoted full title: *Ancient Law: Its Connection with the Early History of Society and Its Relation to Modern Ideas.* By Society the author means specifically Western society, intellectually ancestral to ourselves. Maine's evolutionary ideas were developed neither from mythology nor from comparative ethnography but from ancient history—the earliest known documents from Palestine, Greece, and Rome. ". . . the Homeric literature is far more trustworthy than those relatively later documents that profess to give an account of times similarly early, but which were compiled under philosophical or theological influences. These rudimentary ideas are to the jurist what the primary crusts of the earth are to the geologist. They contain, potentially, all of the forms in which law has subsequently exhibited itself" (Maine 1861, 2-3). The author is consistently critical of those theories resting on logic rather than evidence, which were prevalent in his own time and still remain today. "Theories, plausible and comprehensive, but absolutely unverified . . . enjoy a universal preference over sober research into the primitive history of society and law; they obscure the truth . . . ." (Ibid.).

Ancient Law is in ten chapters, each dealing with a different aspect of law, or its history. The first chapter discusses the nature of the earliest Western legal codes, as they can be deduced from Homer and other archaic sources. The second discusses the phenomenon of legal fictions, which allow the application of law beyond its original intent. Chapters

III and IV both deal with natural law: those aspects of belief that seem to derive from human nature itself.

Chapter V, "Primitive Society and Ancient Law" is the one of most specific interest to us here. In it the author develops two revolutionary themes. One is that the earliest human groupings were based entirely on kinship, not on territoriality. ". . . the idea that a number of persons should exercise political rights in common simply because they happened to live within the same topographical limits was utterly strange and monstrous to primitive antiquity" (Maine 1861, 138). The other is that the primary concern of early law was for kin groups, not individuals. They were essentially corporations: they owned or controlled the land and all other essential resources in common, and they were collectively responsible for all the actions of their members. Hence Maine's most oft-quoted dictum: "ancient law knows next to nothing of individuals" (Maine 1861, 134).

From his studies of law Maine took it as self-evident that the earliest societies were not only patrilineal but patriarchal. A great deal of Chapter V is in fact devoted to citing all kinds of evidence to show that *Patria Potestas,* the granting of absolute and unlimited power of a father over his children, including the power of life and death, was once universal. In larger kin groupings, which were the norm in ancient times, this was extended to mean the power of the headman over his lineage of clan. All the males were, after all, descendants of one common *Pater,* whose authority was inherited by his eldest son, and in turn passed on to his. All the females had been grafted onto the kin group through the legal fiction represented by marriage, and thus became in effect daughters.

Maine's other important theoretical contribution, appearing only at the end of Chapter V, is the idea of social evolution from Status to Contract, or as we would say today, the evolution from ascribed to achieved status. In the earliest societies a person's social position was determined entirely by kinship, and therefore inherited at birth and re-tained throughout life (ascribed); it was non-negotiable. But as extended kin groups decayed, and power flowed more and more to the individual, he had increasing ability to determine his social status through his own actions and contacts (achieved). Though Maine was generally critical of sweeping theories about social evolution, he saw the movement from status to contract as the one universal development.

Subsequent chapters of *Ancient Law* deal successively with wills and inheritance, with property, with contracts, and with crime. The treatment in each case is historical, but does not involve a broad evolutionary perspective.

Village Communities

Maine's other major work, written after his return from India, was *Village Communities East and West* (1871). The title of the work is somewhat misleading, for it is not really ethnographic, and is only incidentally concerned with village life. Like nearly all the works of Maine it is basically a study of the evolution of law. While *Ancient Law* is mainly concerned with social organization and inheritance, however, the main focus of this work is on systems of land tenure, based on a comparison of supposedly ancient and modern practices

In his years as legal advisor to the British imperial government in India, Maine had made a study of the common law of land tenure as practiced by illiterate villagers, and he concluded that it represented a survival of a very early form of law. After return to England he read up on ancient and medieval village law, especially in Germany, and discovered many of the same practices he had observed in India. From those sources he formulated a general model of ancient land law, centering around the idea of the commons (communally owned land which may be used by all members of a group).

Appended to the text of the book are three lectures delivered at the University of Calcutta, having to do with the education of jurists, and various aspects of the practice of law in India; a fairly lengthy essay entitled "The Theory of Evidence," and another entitled "Roman Law and Legal Education." These are of considerable historical interest, though their bearing on the development of anthropological thought is slight.

Maine was a man of wide interests and a fluent pen. Throughout his life he published a considerable number of newspaper and journal articles over a variety of subjects.

Perspective

Ancient Law is far and away the most profound of Maine's books, and gained him both immediate recognition and lasting fame. A measure of its impact can be seen in the fact that it had already reached ten editions, and been translated into French and German, within its author's lifetime. It was to play an important part in every serious discussion of social evolution for the next half century, and some of its issues are still much debated.

Maine was not wholly without detractors. The year 1861, when *Ancient Law* appeared, saw also the publication of *Das Mutterrecht*, with its insistence on primeval matriliny and matriarchy. These were possibilities that never occurred to Maine, basing himself as he did on scripture rather than mythology. But the matrilineal theory proved to have considerable appeal, especially to persons who enjoyed the idea of the promiscuous horde, and some of them became outspoken critics of Maine. The most insistent of them was John McLennan, whose work and ideas will be discussed in the next chapter. It was not in Maine's nature to quarrel openly with his critics;[4] in two later books, *Lectures on the Early History of Institutions* (1875) and *Dissertations on Early Law and Customs* (1883) he merely restated and defended his earlier ideas.

In the end Maine's basic evolutionary theory was undone not by mythology but by ethnography, a field of research that grew rapidly in the latter years of the nineteenth century. Already in his Preface to the Tenth Edition of *Ancient Law* he was obliged to note that ". . . the observation of savage or extremely barbarous races has brought to light forms of social organisation extremely unlike that to which [I have] referred the beginnings of law, and possibly in some cases of greater antiquity" (Maine 1884, vii). Later Lowie (1920) was to show that social groupings not based on kinship (sodalities) are found among many tribal groups, and also that the territorial factor can never be wholly disregarded (Lowie 1927). Still more recent researches among the most primitive bands surviving in the modern world have discovered that

---

[4] He is generally credited with a fairly vitriolic anonymous response of McLennan; see Rivière 1970, xxxvi.

leadership tends to be weakly developed, and situationally conferred rather than inherited; also that descent is very often reckoned through both father and mother (Steward 1955; Lee and Devore 1968).

We know now that Maine was absolutely wrong in taking the early Hebrews as his model of the earliest society (as Bachofen also sometimes did). They offer in reality an example of nomadic pastoral society, which did not exist before the domestication of animals. In the Middle East it survives down to the present day.

Maine's theory of evolution from status to contract has fared some-what better. We know today that it is correct as a general rule, though not without exceptions. In law, all hereditary statuses except those of gender and parentage have indeed disappeared from the most advanced societies. But we also know that some contractual statuses were present in the earliest times. Leadership itself was more often conferred than hereditary, and the shaman represents another obvious example of a conferred status.

CHAPTER FOUR

JOHN MCLENNAN
AND EXOGAMY

John Ferguson McLennan (1827-1881) was born and spent all of his earliest years in Inverness, Scotland, where his father was an insurance agent. In due course he went off to college in Aberdeen, earned a master's degree, and then went on to Cambridge University in England. He apparently excelled in Mathematics, but left the university after two years without completing a degree—probably because he quarreled with his tutors, if his later life is any indication. He remained two more years in the south of England, engaged in literary and journalistic work and hobnobbing with the *literati,* then returned to Scotland to study law. He was admitted to the bar in 1857.

McLennan practiced law in Edinburgh until 1870. Then, after the death of his wife, he gave up his practice and moved permanently to London, where he obtained the post of parliamentary draftsman (i.e. apparently drawing up laws) for Scotland. By this time he had published *Primitive Marriage* (1865) and gained considerable recognition as an armchair ethnologist, and he was elected a member of the Ethnological Society of London immediately upon settling there. But a change of government forced his resignation from his parliamentary position in 1875, and he devoted the remainder of his short life to writing articles. In late years he was in intermittent ill health from tuberculosis, from which he eventually died at the age of 53.

McLennan's was not a satisfying life, in considerable part due to his own contrariness. As his biographer writes, "The bare outlines of McLennan's life are enough to reveal him as a man unable to come to terms with the conventions of the society in which he lived. His failure to achieve success in his legal career and to obtain an academic post may have been a result of his character . . . ." (Rivière 1970, xiii). He is famous among anthropologists for his acerbic quarrel with Maine over the issue of matriliny, but this was only one of his many skirmishes. His dispute with Herbert Spencer over the issue of exogamy was so acrimonious that Spencer was to write "Mr. McLennan has introduced into his rejoinder a tone which renders it undesirable to continue the discussion" (ibid., xix). He described the theories of Lewis Henry Morgan as a "wild dream—not to say nightmare" (Evans-Pritchard 1981, 61). He was caustically critical of his fellow lawyers and even of the law itself. Much of his time in Edinburgh was spent in attempts to change the existing legal system, and for a time he was secretary of the Scottish Society for the Amendment of the Law.

At the same time McLennan had a wide circle of devoted friends, who described him as a "kind and charming companion." An article in the *Encyclopaedia Britannica* described him as having"…a warm and affectionate disposition and [a] readiness to help all workers in science, especially young men of promise" (Rivière 1970, xiv). (For further detail about McLennan's life see Rivière 1970).

Primitive Marriage

It is not known when, or why, McLennan began to study ethnography. By the time he published *Primitive Marriage* he had clearly read a lot of it, for the work introduces far more ethnography than do either Bachofen or Maine. However, this interest is revealed in only one of his previous publications, a review of some works on India published two years earlier (Rivière 1970, xvi-xvii). After *Primitive Marriage* the author continued for the rest of his life to publish articles on anthropological subjects, but his only further anthropological book was published posthumously (McLennan 1885).

Be that as it may, McLennan like Bachofen is remembered entirely for a single book. *Primitive Marriage* (1865) espouses a view on matriliny comparable to that of Bachofen (whose work he had not actually read at the time) and a view on extended kin groups similar to that of Maine, although in due time he was to quarrel with Maine on most other points. To those perspectives he added the concept of exogamy, which was his own unique contribution and the reason for his enduring fame.

Primitive Marriage is labeled by its author as a treatise on bride-capture; its subtitle is *An Inquiry into the Origin of the Form of Capture in Marriage Ceremonies.* This refers to the ritual, indeed common in different forms among many peoples, in which the groom and his adherents pretend to carry off the bride over the resistance of her family. For example, throughout the Middle East it is common for the groom and his pals go in a body to the bride's house, stage a mock raid, and bring her away while her brothers tag along and skirmish with the abductors. Arab friends tell me that after a good wedding there should at least be a couple of black eyes. The final, vestigial survival of the ritual may be seen in the European and American custom of carrying the bride over the threshold.

However, McLennan's treatment of the subject depends on five presuppositions that are really the theoretical meat of the book:

1. Primitive society was strictly matrilineal.
2. Primitive society was organized into extended kin groups.
3. Those groups were always exogamous, meaning that men had to seek their wives from neighboring kin groups.
4. Kin groups were usually hostile to one another, so that brides had to be obtained by capture.
5. That state of affairs is memorialized in the rituals of symbolic bride capture so common in marriage ceremonies today.

Chapter 1 sets out the methodology that Tylor would later call the "doctrine of survivals"—the belief that the seemingly incomprehensible customs and symbols of today are atrophied survivals of ancient actualities (Tylor 1871, Ch. III-IV). Chapter 2 reviews a number of cases in which symbolic bride capture is described in ancient literature, and rejects the suggestions that it was no more than the way to overcome girlish shyness. In Chapter 3 the author offers his own alternative explanation: *that bride capture was necessitated by exogamy.* McLennan would later claim that he invented the terms *exogamy* and *endogamy*, though he did not make that claim in *Primitive Marriage.* He was by no means the first to notice the practice of marrying out, but he was indeed the first to recognize its universality and to make it the basis of his theoretical scheme. Chapters 4-6 are devoted to "proving" the exogamy thesis: first, by showing that there are peoples today who still practice actual bride-capture; second, by showing that all such peoples have a rule of exogamy; third, that war is the normal relationship among primitive peoples.

Chapter 7, on the origin of exogamy, introduces what is by all odds McLennan's most bizarre and controversial theory. He ignores altogether the commonly cited factor of incest taboo; "A survey of the facts of primitive life . . . exclude[s] the notion that the law originated in any innate or primary feeling against marriage with kinsfolk" (McLennan 1970, 58). The explanation lies rather in the "universal" practice of female infanticide among the most primitive peoples. They supposedly killed not just some but all of their female offspring, leaving the males with no alternative but to seek mates elsewhere.

Chapter 8 sounds three themes that to McLennan are basic: first, that the earliest societies were strictly and necessarily matrilineal; second, that shortage of females, through infanticide, led to a general practice of polyandry; third, that society evolved from promiscuous horde through two stages of polyandry to more ordinary matrimony. This is the author's closest approach to an evolutionary schema. Chapter 9 discusses, in rather vague terms, the breakdown of exogamy with the emergence of more advanced societies. The very brief Conclusion (Chapter 10) merely recapitulates the author's main theses *Primitive Marriage* was at best a moderate success, and it created no splash among fellow ethnologists. Its polemical tone, its numerous errors, and its bizarre theories all conspired to mask its virtues, which were recognized by only a few. It must have been particularly galling to McLennan that his work was republished only once in his lifetime, along with other, shorter essays, in a volume called *Studies in Ancient History* (1976). By that time Maine's *Ancient Law* had already undergone six editions.

Later writings

In the years after *Primitive Marriage* McLennan published 14 articles and two books, but not all of them were related to anthropology. Most important among them are five articles discussing the newly hot topic of totemic religion, which had not yet been "discovered" when *Primitive Marriage* was written. McLennan immediately concluded that it was functionally connected with matrilineal descent, an idea that was not widely accepted by the numerous other sages writing on the subject then and later. (Totemism will be much more fully discussed in later pages). In other articles, dealing with exogamy and with polyandry, McLennan restated and defended his earlier positions. (For a listing of all of McLennan's works see Rivière 1970, xlix-xi.)

In his last years McLennan began working collaboratively with his younger brother Donald, also a lawyer, on a book with the title *The Patriarchal Theory*. The senior brother died before completion of the work, which was undertaken by Donald McLennan. It was published in 1885, "based on the papers of the late John Ferguson McLennan."

The Patriarchal Theory is McLennan's parting shot in his lifelong feud with Maine, for the book from end to end is a running critique of the latter's work. Early chapters are devoted to refuting Maine's arguments for the priority of patriarchal authority specifically among the Hebrews, Hindus, Slavs, Irish, and in rules of royal succession. Later chapters are devoted to considering how *agnation* (patrilineal kinship reckoning) came about, while insisting that it is not an essential derivative of patriarchal authority.

Perspective

John McLennan was wrong most of the time, and when he was right it was usually for the wrong reasons. Despite the abundance of ethnographic citations, his use of them was highly selective. In the end his theories, like those of nearly all other social evolutionists then and since, rest basically on logic rather than evidence. Yet drawing on ethnography, rather than on either mythology or scripture, did lead him to discover one of the most fundamental principles of social organization—that of exogamy—which had escaped both Bachofen and Maine. In addition at least some colleagues recognized and appreciated his methodology, even when it led to mistaken conclusions. Tylor described it as the ". . . introduction of the scientific method of induction from observed facts," and an anonymous reviewer even opined that "Mr. McLennan has opened a new path in historical research" (Rivière 1970, xxxvii).

CHAPTER FIVE

LEWIS HENRY MORGAN AND KINSHIP CLASSIFICATION

Lewis Morgan (1818-1881), as he was christened,[5] was one of thirteen children born to a prosperous farmer, inventor, and sometime politician in western New York. The family home was in the small town of Aurora, where Lewis spent most of his youth. The father died when Lewis was eight, but he had left his family well provided for, including funds specifically earmarked for the education of his children. Those funds enabled Lewis to attend Cayuga Academy and then Union College, both in upstate New York. In college he studied classics, as was mandatory in all colleges in those days, but also mechanics and optics, and he developed a strong interest in natural history.

After graduation Morgan returned to Aurora to read law with an established firm; he was admitted to the bar in 1842. In that year he moved to the city of Rochester, New York, which was to be his home for the remainder of his life, and there he opened a law partnership with a Union College classmate. Business was slow at first, with the country in the grip of a recession, but it picked up markedly after 1845, as Rochester grew rapidly through industrial development. In 1851 Morgan married his first cousin, and his financial situation was further solidified when in 1853 she received a large inheritance.

---

[5] He inserted the "Henry" later in life to sound more distinguished.

In later life Morgan followed in his father's footsteps as an active man of affairs with varied interests. He became a corporation lawyer but also invested in railroads, mineral development, and land schemes, and served in the New York State Assembly from 1851 to 1860, and again in 1868-9. By then his investments had made him financially independent, and he could devote his latter years to political activities and increasingly to his ethnological studies, on which his enduring fame would in time rest.

Morgan was ill throughout the year 1881 with a condition that was described as "nervous exhaustion," and he died in December of that year, at the age of 63.

The League of the Iroquois

Morgan throughout his youth had a strong interest in natural history, which in his mind included the native cultures of America.[6] Soon after settling in Rochester he helped organize a group of young *intelligentsia* into a literary and debating society originally calling itself The Gordian Knot. Its focus was on the reading and discussion of the classics. A year or so later however Morgan decided that the society should refocus itself entirely on the study of Native American culture and society, and it was renamed The Grand Order of the Iroquois, later changed to the New Confederacy of the Iroquois. The members began to call each other *sachem* (an Algonkian word for "chief") instead of "Mister;" they paraded in Indian costume and met around campfires in the summer.

The Grand Order were little more than a bunch of Boy Scouts playing Indian until, in 1844, a chance encounter changed the direction of Morgan's life. Browsing in an Albany bookstore, he met an educated young Seneca (i.e. Iroquois) Indian, Ely Parker, who had come to Albany, the state capital, along with a delegation of tribal elders, to negotiate for tribal rights. Morgan fell into conversation with the young man and was invited by him to come to a hotel room and meet the elders. Absolutely fascinated by what he learned, he interviewed them that evening and

---

[6] An interest that would lead, among many other things, to the publication of a book, *The American Beaver and His Works* (1868).

again the next day and the next, and came away with reams of notes. From that moment on ethnology was for him a serious business. "The tribesmen explained the organization of the Iroquois Confederacy, the structure of a tribe and clan, and supplied him with relevant Seneca terms. In this chance encounter American ethnology was born" (Resek 1960, 27).

Ely[7] S. Parker was an extraordinary individual who in time would have a distinguished career of his own. His people had raised money to send him to school and to study law so that he could defend their interests in court, against white encroachment. It then turned out that, as a non-citizen, he was barred from practicing law in New York. (Indians did not become U.S. citizens until 1924.) But he did in time make several visits to Washington to lobby for Indian interests before both the president and the congress, and impressed both with his eloquence.

Barred from practicing law, Parker turned to civil engineering and, after graduating from Rensselaer Polytechnic Institute, got several commissions designing both canals and buildings. One commission was to built a customs house at Galena, Illinois, and while there he became friends with retired U.S. Army Captain Ulysses Grant, then living in the town. When Grant was recalled to military service at the start of the Civil War he wangled a commission for his Indian friend to serve as his aide-de-camp. Throughout the war Parker wrote many of the general's dispatches, and it was he who drew up the articles of Confederate surrender at Appomattox. He was mustered out with the rank of brigadier general. A little later, when Grant was elected president, he appointed Parker to the post of Commissioner for Indian affairs—the only Indian to hold that office for more than a hundred years. Parker ended his career in the office of the New York City police commissioner. (For a biography of Ely Parker see Anderson 1978.)

All that lay far in the future when the sixteen-year-old Parker met Morgan for the first time in 1844. It was a future that Morgan himself did much to shape. He invited Parker to lecture to the Grand Order of the Iroquois, and then to join it, which brought the young Indian into

---

[7] Pronounced E-lee.

contact with important businessmen. Later it was the members of the Order who paid for Parker's education as an engineer, and it was Morgan who got him his first job. Meanwhile all the time Morgan kept querying him, and other tribal members, about the customs of the Seneca. If Morgan in time became the first American ethnologist, Ely Parker was assuredly the first anthropological informant.

Morgan's interest was piqued above all by the League of the Iroquois, a grouping without precedent in Native America. It was a formally organized confederacy of six (originally five) independent tribes, with formal rules for meeting, voting, and the like. The Seneca were one of the six tribes. Americans had long known of the existence of the confederacy, but knew nothing in detail about its constitution. Morgan in due time wrote his first book about it (Morgan 1851), and it remains to this day one of the primary sources of information about the League. It was the first true American ethnography, and it permanently established the author's standing as an ethnologist. It also led to his election to the American Association for the Advancement of Science.

Systems of Consanguinity and Affinity

Morgan was also intrigued, and surprised, by the Iroquois system of naming kinsmen, which was quite different from the Euro-American system. Mother and her sister were alike called "mother," father and his brother were alike called "father," and the offspring of those "mothers" and "fathers" (technically parallel cousins) were called brothers and sisters. Morgan read a paper on the Iroquois kinship system before the American Association for the Advancement of Science in 1859. Then, while on a business trip to Michigan, he discovered that the Ojibwa Indians (otherwise known as Chippewa) employed the same system of kin terminology as that of the Iroquois. He supposed at first that it must be pan-Indian, but inquiries among Indian agents and missionaries soon showed him otherwise. It turned out that there were many different ways of classifying kin.

A whole new avenue of research opened up for Morgan, and it was to occupy him off and on for the rest of his life. Contemporary social theorists like Maine and McLennan had been writing knowledgeably about kinship, but they had never interested themselves in the question of kin nomenclature because they had never been near an actual tribesman. Morgan persuaded the Smithsonian Institution to sponsor him in a program of comparative study of the subject that would eventually involve four field trips to the western Indians, and questionnaires sent to missionaries and others around the world. Morgan himself collected kin terms from 51 different tribes. The upshot, in 1871, was the publication of *Systems of Consanguinity and Affinity of the Human Family,* a massive tome of more than 600 quarto-size pages, including dozens of pages of comparative tables.

Morgan distinguished at the outset between what he called descriptive and classificatory systems. Descriptive systems were those that distinguished relatives only be generation and sex, as in Europe and America, while classificatory systems introduced more complex bases of differentiation or grouping, as among the Iroquois.

In the broadest terms, Morgan believed that kinship nomenclature generally co-varied with language. That is, languages in any given family were likely to employ the same kinship nomenclature, and this furnished the organizational basis for *Systems of Consanguinity.* Part I is devoted to the enumeration of descriptive systems as found in the Aryan (Indo-European), Semitic, and Uralian (Ural-Altaic) language families, found over much of the Eurasian continent. Part II enumerates classificatory systems as found in what Morgan calls the Ganowánian family, which embraced all Native American peoples. Part III enumerates classificatory systems among the "Turanian" and Malayan families. Turanian like Ganowánian was a term invented by Morgan, to include Chinese, Dravidian, and certain languages of India.

Systems of Consanguinity and Affinity presented a truly prodigious amount of raw data, but its theoretical significance was debatable from the start. Morgan was no linguist, and his classification of language families came in for abundant criticism in his own time. Considerable variability of Native American languages had already been recognized before his time, and we now know that there is enormous variability among them, including at least six totally independent stocks. We know also that Chinese belongs to a very large family (Sino-Tibetan) but has no relationship to Dravidian. Co-variance of language family and kin nomenclature has proved to be much more true in some families than in others. And the distinction between classificatory and descriptive systems has not proved useful, because most systems have aspects of both.

Morgan's primary theoretical conviction, which provided the motivation for his studies, was that recurrence of any kinship system among different peoples must be evidence of a common origin, at some point back in time. This idea, if not wholly disproven, was at least very much at variance with his own distributional data; e.g. the occurrence of the Iroquoian system in south India. Yet the extraordinarily discontinuous distribution of many kinship systems, around the world, remains to this day difficult to account for on any other basis.

What has survived from Morgan's labors is the recognition of seven recurring systems of kinship nomenclature that occur around the world: Iroquoian, Crow, Omaha, Eskimo, Hawaiian, Sudanese, and Dravidian. These have become part of the standard vocabulary of social anthropology. The first three of the systems bear Native American names because they were discovered by Morgan's own labors, but they are found in many other parts of the world as well.

Ancient Society

At the time when he wrote *Systems of Consanguinity* Morgan was a diffusionist, not an evolutionist. He wanted to see his recurring systems of kinship reckoning as evidence of common origin, not of evolutionary development. But his contemporaries Bachofen, Maine, and McLennan had all linked their discoveries about kinship unhesitatingly to evolutionary stage theory, and it was perhaps inevitable that Morgan too would be drawn into that discourse. He was drawn in initially not by the reading of other works but by his own ethnographic researches, which had convinced him of the basic sameness of all American Indians (his Ganowánian Family). This was best explained in his mind as an evolutionary stage.

Evolutionary stage theory was nothing new. It had been around since ancient Greek times, and had been quite fully elaborated by thinkers of the French and Scottish Enlightenments. Adam Ferguson had even named his three evolutionary stages savagery, barbarism, and civilization—the terms later borrowed and made famous by Morgan (see Adams 1998, 12-26). But the Enlightenment sages, like Bachofen, Maine and McLennan who came after them, lacked any ethnographic grounding; their schemes were based very largely on logic.

Morgan, as an American, had two huge advantages over his fellows. First, he commanded a prodigious amount of ethnographic data from his own researches; he did not have to rely strictly on books. Second, like most Americans, he was an out-and-out materialist, with an extensive knowledge of technology into the bargain. He was able to give his evolutionary theory a far more explicit material grounding then had any other theorist of the time, or most since then. His studies came to fruition in *Ancient Society,* published in 1877. The book has the subtitle *Researches in the Lines of Human Progress from Savagery through Barbarism to Civilization.*

The sources of inspiration for Morgan's evolutionism are far from clear, given that there is no more than a hint of it in *Systems of Consanguinity.* It could be said that social evolutionism was simply in the air among the *intelligentsia;* this was the time when it was replacing diffusion as the preferred explanation for cultural similarities. A number of contemporaries who had read and admired *Systems,* including such luminaries as Darwin, Huxley, Spencer, and Lubbock, had assured him that his kinship studies had clear evolutionary implications.

Morgan's basic evolutionary schema envisions the three basic stages of Savagery, Barbarism, and Civilization, of which the first two have three sub-stages. The whole schema is set forth in brief at the very outset of *Ancient Society* (Morgan 1877, 9-12). The Lower Status of Savagery was a time when mankind "subsisted on fruits and nuts," the Middle Status of Savagery was inaugurated by the development of fire-making and of fishing; the Upper Status of Savagery was inaugurated by the invention of the bow and arrow. The Lower Status of Barbarism saw the invention of pottery; the Middle Status of Barbarism began with both animal domestication and agriculture; the Upper Status of Barbarism was inaugurated by the development of iron smelting. Civilization came with the introduction of the phonetic alphabet.

In *Ancient Society,* the bulk of Part I elaborates on the evolution of material culture, which Morgan saw as the stimulus for human mental ability: "growth of intelligence through inventions and discoveries." The very long Part II is devoted to the "growth of the idea of government," with four chapters just on the Iroquois. Part III, "growth of the idea of the family" is the part that relates most clearly back to his earlier work on kinship, as well as that of Bachofen, Maine, and McLennan, all of whom are quoted. Morgan goes along with Bachofen and McLennan on the subject of matrilineal priority. The most novel but surely the most controversial part of this section is its last chapter, in which the author arranges his different systems of kinship nomenclature into a developmental sequence. This is admitted to be hypothetical, and in fact it gained almost no adherents, then or since. The fourth, brief section is on the "growth of the idea of property."

Ancient Society clearly went far beyond any evolutionary schema previously proposed. It gained an immediate, very wide audience, and soon made its author world famous. As a starting point for all future discussion it was to social evolution what *The Origin of Species* was to biological evolution. Henry Adams wrote that it must become "the foundation for all future work in American historical science;" Herbert Spencer regretted that it was not published soon enough for his own use in *Principles of Sociology"* (Resek 1960, 141-2).

It is obvious today that Morgan's scheme contains a host of errors, both factual and theoretical. For the factual errors the author can hardly be blamed; they reflect the universal ignorance of an age when both ethnology and prehistoric archaeology were just getting started. Ethnology would show in time that the theory of matrilineal priority was untenable; that clans were by no means universal in primitive society, and that there were very advanced societies, in northwestern America, having neither pottery nor agriculture. Archaeology would reveal even more basic deficiencies. Morgan had assumed that hunting began with the bow and arrow; thousands of spear point finds, as well as cave paintings, were to show that humans were already hunting millennia earlier. Morgan fixed the invention of pottery well before the development of agriculture, while excavations in the Near East have demonstrated that the two originated almost simultaneously. He followed several earlier sages, including Ferguson and Millar, in postulating a pastoral stage preceding the first agriculture; we know today that the earliest domestication of plants preceded the domestication of animals, except for the dog. Morgan very much overestimated the importance of fishing and of iron smelting, and underestimated the importance of bronze and of the wheel.

Problems of another sort arose when Morgan sought to put pigeons into his pigeonholes. It was one thing to formulate, in the abstract, an elegant scheme of developmental stages; it was quite another to fit actual people into them. It turned out that quite a few peoples are simple in some respects and complex in others. Above all Morgan was the victim of his lifelong conviction that all American Indians—even the Aztecs and Maya—were at roughly the same stage of development. When the complexity of Aztec civilization was pointed out to him, Morgan insisted that it had been very much exaggerated by the conquistadores for their own self-glorification. He went so far as to publish a rather sarcastic article on the subject, with the title "Montezuma's Dinner" (Morgan 1876).

Some of these deficiencies had been pointed out in Morgan's own time. McLennan was severely critical, and Tylor asserted "that the author has built up a structure of theory, wider and heavier than his foundation of fact will bear" (Resek 1960, 142). Yet no one came right out to criticize what is clearly the most fundamental weakness of the scheme: its absurd simplicity. It was in that respect a product of its time: a smugly confident age when triumphant Science was finding order in the complexities of both nature and history, and would soon answer all questions.

It was that very simplicity that gave *Ancient Society* such immortality as it still enjoys. Karl Marx and Friedrich Engels had set out to formulate their own evolutionary scheme, beginning with the earliest times and ending with the utopian worker's paradise. Lacking any concrete information, they were at a loss how to write the earliest chapter until they discovered that Morgan had written it for them. *Ancient Society* was forthwith adopted as one of Marxism's "sacred texts," and it was required reading for all enrolled Communists for more than a century. As a result, as Lowie (1937, 54) remarks, ". . . German workingmen would sometimes reveal an uncanny familiarity with the Hawaiian and Iroquois mode of designating kin, matters not obviously connected with a proletarian revolution." Reading the work was still required for party members in China when I was teaching there in the 1980s, and a colleague told me he was very much disturbed to find that the primitive hill tribe he had been studying did not practice matrilineal inheritance. The ultimate irony is that Morgan himself was an unabashed capitalist, and his book has even been called by some an apologia for capitalism.

Archaeology at last

In the summer of 1878 Morgan took a vacation trip through southern Colorado and New Mexico, accompanied by a nephew with a keen archaeological interest. They visited both puebloan ruins and living pueblos, and Morgan found a new field in interest. On his return he read two papers on southwestern Indian architecture, and he began a new book embracing all Indian architecture. Characteristically for him, he was not impressed by its diversity but rather found that all the different kinds of buildings gave evidence of primitive communism. "The pueblos proved conclusively . . . that the primitive family could survive only as part of a larger household . . . ." (Resek 1970, 147). In a way, of course, he was only confirming archaeologically what Maine had said about the corporate kin group. *Houses and House-Life of the American Indians* appeared as a large and profusely illustrated volume in 1881, under the aegis of the U.S. Geographical and Geological Survey West of the Rocky Mountains.

Belatedly, Morgan became an enthusiast for archaeology. He joined the newly founded Archaeological Institute of America, and drew up for it a thirty-page proposal for a study of Indian architecture from New Mexico to Panama. It was at least partly at Morgan's suggestion that the Archaeological Institute funded Adolph Bandelier to begin its first program of excavation in New Mexico.

Perspective

Lewis Henry Morgan is much better remembered, at least in America, than Bachofen, Maine, or McLennan, for in addition to scholarly activity he was very much a man of action. His prodigious energies contributed to both anthropology and Indian studies in a variety of ways. In the beginning, his legal work on behalf of the Seneca resulted eventually in the recovery of their reservation, and to his adoption into the tribe.

Together with Ely Parker, he did much to promote the assimilationist Indian policy adopted by President Grant and all later presidents for half a century. This is widely condemned today, but there was really no other alternative for the Plains Indians once the buffalo were gone. Because of his towering reputation, Morgan's belated enthusiasm for archaeology was an important factor in stimulating field studies, especially in the Southwest.

Morgan certainly devoted more effort to *Systems of Consanguinity and Affinity* than to all his other works combined, but it was to be the least influential of them. It was not issued in a large edition, and copies are very rare today. Such importance as it had lay not in its content but simply in making anthropologists aware of a previously unsuspected domain of cultural variability And the massive comprehensiveness of the volume conveyed the suggestion that the subject must be important. No ethnologist for the next half century would study a tribe or village without recording its kinship system. Yet the question remains to this day: what does it tell us about anything other than itself?

The great A. L. Kroeber, after studying kinship at Zuni, was convinced that kinship nomenclature was nothing more than linguistic data. His colleague Robert Lowie, studying the culturally similar pueblos of Hopi, considered it importantly connected with land tenure.

Ancient Society, like McLennan's kinship theories, is wrong in much of its content, but in the development of evolutionary theory it has an importance that far transcends its content. There is first of all its comprehensiveness: it offers a single evolutionary theory embracing all the different aspects of culture except (conspicuously) religion. (He had written that ". . . all primitive religions are grotesque and to some extent unintelligible:" Morgan 1877, 5-6). Even more important is the fact that it established, apparently for all time, the idea that material and technical progress is the driving force of cultural evolution. This has been ever since the basic principle of all Euro-American evolutionary schemes.

CHAPTER SIX

E. B. TYLOR, CULTUROLOGY
AND ANIMISM

Edward Burnett Tylor (1832-1917) was born in London, into a wealthy family that owned a brass foundry. The family's Quaker religion at the time precluded young Tylor's entry into a major university, and instead, at age 16, he went directly into the family business. He worked there for seven years, but in 1855 a diagnosis of suspected tuberculosis caused him to take a trip to the Caribbean and Mexico. There he made the acquaintance of a distinguished amateur archaeologist and ethnologist (and fellow Quaker), Henry Christy, who became his guide and mentor. As a result, Tylor came back from his trip determined to pursue the study of anthropology.

Not long after his return he published his first book, *Anahuac* (1861), based on his travels in Mexico. He never returned to the family business, but nevertheless lived on income from it for the next 25 years. Like Darwin—also supported by a family business—he stayed at home, studied, and wrote two seminal books (1865 and 1871). A decade later, still without any teaching position, he wrote the first out-and-out anthropology textbook, simply titled *Anthropology* (1881). Then in 1884, at the somewhat advanced age of 52, he was appointed Reader in Anthropology at Oxford, but his Quaker religion prevented his promotion to Professor until the Oxford "religious tests" were removed in 1895. By that time, thanks to his position as Britain's first professor of anthropology, as well as his several books, Anthropology had come to be widely regarded as

"Mr. Tylor's science" (Kardiner and Preble 1961, 76). He was very belatedly knighted at the age of 80, in 1912.

Culturology

Bachofen, Maine, and McLennan were all, strictly speaking, sociologists; their theories never extended beyond the domain of social organization. Morgan was more nearly a social anthropologist, insofar as his theories embraced all the domains of culture except religion. For him as much as the others, however, social development was the driving force of evolution; other aspects of culture were more or less dependent variables. If they used the term "culture" at all, it had no theoretical significance.

At the same time, German ethnologists were embracing "culture," rather than "society," as the central organizing concept of their discipline. This perception sprang quite simply from the special circumstances of Germany as a nation without a state. The Germans, no less than other Europeans, had been swept by the radical new ideology of nationalism at the beginning of the modern age, but unlike their neighbors they had not achieved a unified nation-state. Bismarck had attempted to create one in 1870, but Austria had declined to join, and Switzerland and the Sudetenland were also left out. In the hands of nationalists like Wagner, Germanness was a matter or great pride, but it was based entirely on culture and language, not on owing allegiance to anyone or belonging to anything. German achievements were in the arts, literature and philosophy, not on the battlefield or in the corridors of power. And as they defined themselves strictly in cultural terms, so the Germans applied the same measure to other peoples (see Adams 1998, 263-4).

On this point Tylor's outlook was wholly German; that is, he was a cultural determinist through and through. Note that his *magnum opus* has the title *Primitive Culture*, while that of Morgan is named *Ancient Society*. How Tylor came by his culturological outlook in not entirely clear. In writing his two most important books he drew very extensively on German ethnographic literature, for there was nothing comparable in any other language. Everything suggests however that his perspective was already developed long before he began to write. Most likely it grew out of his cross-cultural experiences in Mexico, which were far more extensive than those of any predecessors. Bachofen and McLennan had no direct experience with alien cultures; Maine had dealt only with the literate and complex society of India, and Morgan's ethnographic encounters, while numerous, had been with reservation Indians far removed from their traditional lifeways. Tylor had seen unadulterated culture, on its home ground, in Mexico.

Tylor did not invent the term culture, but he was the first, in English, to make it a basic organizing concept. He also offered the first definition in English: " . . . the complex whole of . . . capabilities and habits acquired by man as a member of society" (Tylor 1871, 1). It was however the German-born Franz Boas and his largely German-American students who were to make it the heart and core of American anthropology for more than a century (Adams 1998, 317).

Researches into the Early History of Mankind

Nine years after his return from Mexico Tylor published the first fruit of his ethnographic and theoretical studies, with the title *Researches into the Early History of Mankind* and the subtitle *and the Development of Civilization* (Tylor 1865). It offered from beginning to end an evolutionary schema, but a very different one from that of Morgan. Where Morgan's day-to-day involvement in financial and industrial affairs made him inevitably a materialist, Tylor's serene detachment from everyday affairs, and dedication to the life of the mind, gave him a much more mentalist outlook. This is proclaimed explicitly in the subtitle to his later book, *Primitive Culture* (1871): *Researches into the development of mythology, philosophy, religion, language, art, and custom*, which could just as well have been the subtitle also of the earlier *Researches into the Early History of Mankind*.

Evolution as seen by Tylor was very much a matter of the collective maturation of the human mind, which he likened to the maturation of an individual person's mind from childhood of adulthood. In each case there were recognizable stages of development, as any parent can attest. In Tylor's view, the stages of maturation were marked above all by an increasing ability to communicate through symbols. Thus the successive chapters of *Researches:* Gesture-Language, Gesture-Language and Word-Language, Picture Writing and Word-Writing, Images and Names, Growth and Decline of Culture, Historical Traditions and Myths of Observation, and Geographical Distribution of Myths. The volume then concludes with an extraordinary, and extraordinarily detailed, chapter on methods of fire-making and cooking, whose inclusion in this work has never been explained.

In developing his evolutionary theories Tylor relied heavily on what he called the "doctrine of survivals," holding that primitive customs in today's world are reliable evidence of earlier evolutionary stages, which have persisted like cultural fossils. Scholars since the time of Locke (1690, 383) had assumed as much, but Tylor was the first to spell it out explicitly as a research methodology. Another of his basic assumptions was "the psychic unity of man," holding that all human minds functioned in the same way, and in similar circumstances would come up with similar solutions to similar problems. Although he did not say it in so many words, this was his refutation of diffusionist theories asserting that cultural parallels could only be evidence of diffusion from a common source.

Primitive Culture

In the course of his studies, Tylor became more and more convinced that the key to understanding human cognitive evolution lay in the study of religion, a topic that had been almost wholly neglected by his predecessors. He could see that religion had progressed through successive stages, each redefining the relationship between the natural and the spiritual worlds. Already hinted at in the latter chapters of *Researches,* this became virtually the *leitmotiv* of his second major work, *Primitive Culture,* published in two volumes in 1871. It was to be far and away his most influential work, and the one on which his lasting reputation rests.

Tylor's definition of religion was short and simple: "belief in spiritual beings" (Tylor 1871, 424). Typically for him, he defines religion entirely in cognitive terms (i.e. belief), and his whole evolutionary schema rests on this presupposition. A fair number of anthropologists have followed him in this, but an equal number have insisted that behavior (ritual) is the defining feature, and still others argue that a special kind of emotion is what sets religion apart from the rest of culture (for extended discussion see Adams 2005, 136-141). This disagreement at the very outset has plagued the development of theories about religion to the present day.

Always a seeker after rationalistic explanations, Tylor believed that religion arose in the first instance out of people's need to explain dreams and trances. As such it found its first expression in mythology—tales which served to give definition and characterization to the myriad causative forces at work in the world around us. These were not in the beginning supernatural forces, for Tylor held that in early thinking there was no division between the natural and the supernatural.

But myths were innumerable and idiosyncratic; separate for each tribe, often for each community, and sometimes for each individual. The first stage of religious development common to all people was that which Tylor named *animism*. The term was not actually coined by him; it had been employed by biologists as an explanation for disease more than a century earlier. Tylor however refocused it as a specifically anthropological concept, relating to religion, and it has remained so ever since.

Tylor's definition of animism, typically for him, was brief and simple: "the general doctrine of souls and other spiritual beings in general" and "an idea of pervading life and will in nature" (Tylor 187, 260). Put in the simplest terms, animism is the ultimate anthropocentrism—the belief that everything in nature, animate and inanimate, has a spirit and a will just as we humans do, and is capable of acting on the world around it just as we are. That spirit and will can be indwelling within each animal, plant, and object, but can also exist outside it, and survive it. In Tylor's evolutionary schema this idea was extended first to animals, then also to plants, and eventually to everything—ultimately to the forces of nature themselves. Thus in time there emerges a belief in a kind of super-spirit, embodying in itself, for example, the spirit of all bears or all pine trees. These being are always present in the surrounding environment, but they dwell simultaneously in a kind of remote Valhalla, which may be on the earth or above it or below it.

Animism for Tylor is the heart and soul of primitive religion, and occupies the predominant place in Volume 2 of *Primitive Culture*. Note once again that it is a purely cognitive concept; religion is defined by what people believe, not by what they do. Rites and ceremonies are dealt with rather briefly in the volume, and relate entirely to collective performances. There is no mention of shamanism, which some scholars consider to be the most essential feature of primitive religion (e.g. Radin 1937). The later stages of religious evolution, involving the development first of polytheism and then of monotheism, are dealt with only summarily by Tylor, and not very persuasively. They had virtually no influence on subsequent theoretical developments. On the other hand the concept of animism as the earliest form of human religious belief became firmly embedded in the anthropological discourse, and has remained so ever since.

Long after Tylor's time, the great Swiss experimental psychologist Jean Piaget was able to show that animistic beliefs are virtually universal in children in all cultures, up to about age 6 (Piaget 1960). Thus, in a way, Piaget seems to confirm Tylor's view that primitive culture represents the childhood of mankind. (For extended discussion see Adams 2005, 307-12).

Kinship theory

Tylor did not wholly ignore social organization; he simply did not give it an important place in his evolutionary schemes. But in his survey of ethnographic data on social organization he became interested in what he called "adhesions," which we now would call correlations. Among the numerous manifestations of kinship-determined behavior, such as inheritance, residence, naming practices, avoidances, and the like, he became interested in discovering "what went with what." His predecessors were prone to intuitive conclusions, such as the correlation of matrilocal residence with matrilineal inheritance, but Tylor insisted in subjecting them all to statistical testing, drawing on his vast archive of ethnographic data. His methodology and results were not published in any of his major books, but in an 1889 article.

Among many other things, Tylor found that avoidances correlated fairly strongly with residence. "There is a well-marked preponderance indicating that ceremonial avoidance by the husband of the wife's family is in some way connected with his living with them, and vice versa as to the wife and the husband's family" (Tylor 1889, 247). He coined the word *teknonymy* for the practice of naming a parent after his child, and found that this correlated with the practice of matrilocal residence. Tylor concluded that many of his "adhesions" supported the then-current belief in evolution from matrilineal to patrilineal kinship, though he did not insist strongly on this as has Bachofen and McLennan. He concluded his article with the assertion that "The key to the position is . . . that in statistical investigation, the future of anthropology lies" (quoted in Evans-Pritchard 1981, 94). (For much fuller discussion of this aspect of Tylor's work see *Ibid.)*

Perspective

Tylor's two main books, *Researches* and *Primitive Culture* both present evolutionary scenarios, and for that reason the author is always counted among the early evolutionary theorists. But in fact Tylor was always averse to grand theorizing, and his evolutionary schemes were presented somewhat modestly, as descriptive rather than prescriptive. Like Boas and Lowie after him, he was a lover of the particular more than of the big picture. Ethnographic facts, however mundane, were like gems to be collected, prized—and displayed. A reviewer of *Primitive Culture* wrote that "What one notes above all is the abundance of documents [i.e. ethnographic examples]. One finds them by piles, by heaps, by mountains, and when these are cleared there are still others" (quoted in Lowie 1937, 83). For that very reason Tylor, again like Boas and Lowie, was dubious of sweeping theories; he could always think of a counter-example to refute them.

Tylor's rather simplified evolutionary schemes have stood up no better to ethnographic inquiry than have the others of his time. Religion in particular has proven a far more difficult subject to grasp than Tylor had supposed; so much so that few subsequent anthropologists have done much better. One has only to look at the enormous diversity of definitions they have offered (see Adams 2005, 136-140), to recognize that religion for anthropologists is very much in the eye of the beholder. Few peoples have any such word, and in their study of other peoples observers have decided for themselves what is and is not religion amid the complex tangle of beliefs, behaviors, and feelings they encounter. (Morgan had anticipated this when he wrote that "The growth of religious ideas is environed with such difficulties that it may never receive a perfectly satisfactory exposition;" Morgan 1877, 5). The definition offered by most scholars generally turns out to be an extended description of a particular religion that they have happened to study.

Like all the other armchair anthropologists of his time, Tylor was an outsider in that he had had no personal contacts with primitive culture. In the study of religion however he was an outsider in another respect as well: he was not himself religious, nor did he grow up in a religious household. Missing altogether from his analysis is any mention of the emotional or mystical components which are for many the chief attractions of religion. To the ever-rationalistic Tylor, religion was simply a system of explanation which made the experienced world intelligible. Other scholars then and since been prone to ignore this function of religion, but Tylor overstressed it. As I have suggested elsewhere, religion may perform so many different functions in different societies and for different individuals that it simply cannot be defined on the basis of its functions (Adams 2005, 181-201).

Tylor deserves enduring credit not for his specific theory of religion but simply for introducing the topic into the anthropological discourse, where nearly all of his predecessors had ignored it. And more specifically, animism remains basic in the conceptual vocabulary of every anthropologist.

From the standpoint of theory, Tylor must be seen today as a giant who left no footprint. His work and views had a considerable impact on his immediate successors, Marett, Rivers, and Haddon among others, but then came the charismatic Malinowski and the dogmatic Radcliffe-Brown. Between them they completely transformed British anthropology, shifting its field of vision from the past to the present, and offering functionalist theories that made both evolution and diffusion irrelevant. The influence of Radcliffe Brown, in particular, was in time sufficient to make British anthropology as wholly sociological as it had been in the days of Maine and McLennan.

The culturological perspective lasted much longer in America, thanks to the work of Franz Boas and his students. However, they drew their influence from German models rather than from Tylor. Moreover, they were as opposed to evolutionary theory as were the Germans; they preferred to attribute all culture growth to diffusion. Evolutionary theory in time has enjoyed a considerable comeback in America, but it is in all respects the materialist evolution of Morgan, not the mentalist evolution of Tylor.

CHAPTER SEVEN

ANDREW LANG AND TOTEMISM

Andrew Lang (1844-1912) was born in Selkirk, Scotland, the son of the town clerk. All of his early education was in Scotland, but he went on eventually to Bailiol College, Oxford, where he concentrated especially on the classics. After graduation he remained for some time as a tutor at Oxford, but then abandoned academia altogether for a full-time career as a writer and independent scholar. By all accounts he was eminently successful in both enterprises.

Lang presents to our eyes a classic example of a now-extinct species: the all-around man of letters once known as a "literary lion." In the course of half a century he wrote a truly prodigious number of books on an equally prodigious variety of subjects, including history, biography, classics, anthropology, religion, psychic research, literary criticism, novels, and poetry. These works, as the subjects suggest, were aimed at an audience of the *literati,* not at the masses more broadly. In addition however he co-wrote with his wife a dozen volumes of fairytales for children.

Lang published five books that were basically anthropological in content. The first two of them (1884 and 1887) were primarily concerned with myth, and were undoubtedly stimulated by his university studies of the classics. He was perhaps also stimulated by Tylor, to whom the 1884 volume is dedicated. Later works however were increasingly concerned with the relationship between religion and society, and here the author broke genuinely fresh ground. Bachofen, Maine, McLennan and Morgan had all formulated social evolutionary schemes that ignored religion; Tylor propounded a religious evolutionary scheme that largely ignored society. Lang was the first to connect the two, through the newly discovered phenomenon of *totemism*. This is a particular system of belief in which each clan on lineage or other kin group worships its own tutelary deity—most commonly an animal; less commonly a plant; still less commonly a natural phenomenon—which is claimed to be ancestral to the group. There is thus established a relationship between a particular kind of religion and a particular kind of social organization.

Totemism: revelation and revolution

Social thinkers from Locke to Morgan had taken the North American Indians as exemplifying the earliest and most primitive forms of culture and society. "The zero of human society," Morgan had called them (quoted in Adams 2005, 59). Then, near the end of the nineteenth century, came the first ethnographic reports on native Australians, and their impact on anthropological thinking was nothing less than revolutionary. Here were people who wore no clothes, built no houses, planted no crops, and used only the crudest of tools and weapons, and they immediately supplanted the North American as everyone's idea of the most primitive living people (see Ibid., and Burridge 1973).

And as their religion was nothing if not totemic, this must surely be the primeval form of human religious belief. In time Frazer (1910), Durkheim (1912) and Freud (1913) were all to write learned books based on that logical but mistaken conclusion. They were however anticipated by Lang, who first raised the suggestion in 1885.

Lang's views on totemism and evolution evolved over time. They were first set forth in the next-to-last chapter of *Custom and Myth* (1884), a book which is largely a compilation of myths. Near the end however the author unexpectedly departs from this theme to discuss "The Early History of the Family." Here he criticizes in detail the patriarchal theory of Maine, and to a lesser extent some of the ideas of Morgan. For the most part he sides with his fellow Scot McLennan (whom he always calls M'Lennan) on the subjects of matrilineal descent, female infanticide, and polyandry.

Totemism is introduced in the analysis only in a modest way, the author demonstrating only that it correlates with exogamy—something that was never in doubt. Totemic practice, as adduced in this volume, provides no support for McLennan's ideas about matriliny, female infanticide, or polyandry. Lang makes what he himself acknowledges is a relatively weak case for the idea that totemism was once a universal evolutionary stage. He does so by citing a fair number of instances of its practice among the "Aryan" race, and suggesting that if it was practiced by this "strong" (his word) race, it must surely have been practiced by weaker races as well (Lang 1884, 272-5).

The Secret of the Totem

Lang's final thoughts on totemism are set forth in *The Secret of the Totem* (1905). The title carries a suggestion of mysticism, but the work is anything but. Like all the anthropological works of Lang, it is drily, not to say tediously, didactic from end to end. The whole volume is devoted to a single issue: the origin of totemism. The "secret" in question was simply the new ethnographic information from Australia that was seemingly being ignored by everyone else. Lang had by this time immersed himself thoroughly in this information, and he cited it repeatedly, in chapter after chapter, to attack various ideas of Maine, Morgan, Darwin, Durkheim, Frazer, and even the Australian ethnographers themselves. He attacked in particular the then popular idea of primitive promiscuity, even though he had earlier written that ". . . the girls of savage tribes are notoriously profligate and immodest about sexual connections" (Lang 1884, 253). Yet he continued to embrace the popular belief in matrilineal priority, while no longer offering any explanation for it.

Lang did break fresh ground in pointing out two facts that at the time were virtually heretical among anthropologists. One was that native Australian religion and society were not nearly as primitive as they had been painted, and should not be taken as models for the earliest human cultural forms. Europeans and Americans, measuring progress purely in material times, had simply been misled by the primitive technology of the Australians. Lang's useful corrective was far too long ignored by fellow anthropologists; Durkheim and Frazer as well as many others clung to the belief that everything started in Australia. It was not until the ¡Kung Bushmen were "discovered" fifty years later that they displaced the Australians as everyone's model of primordial society (see Adams 1998, 68-70). Lang's other corrective observation was that there was a lot of variability in native Australian society, including the presence of both matrilineal and patrilineal tribes. Yet the author remained wholly wedded to the unilinear model of evolution common at the time; he could account for variations in Australian culture only by assuming that they represented differing stages of evolution.

By far the largest part of *The Secret of the Totem* is devoted to attacking other people's theories—always a favorite occupation of Lang. In Chapter VI however he finally gets around to setting forth his own not very convincing theory: that kin groups found it necessary to come up with some kind of supernatural rationale for the names that they had long ago been given, and whose origin had been forgotten (Lang 1905, 111-41).

That Lang should have devoted a whole book to the origin of a single religious belief must be understood in light of the fact that at the time totemism was the hottest topic in anthropology. It was also the case that the armchair anthropologists were obsessed with the search for cultural origins. Today we can recognize that the origins of totemism, lost in the mists of remote antiquity, are no more discoverable than are the origins of most other religious beliefs.

Perspective

In the opening pages of *Custom and Myth* we find an unexpected apology: "I must apologise for the controversial matter in the volume. Controversy is always a thing to be avoided . . ." (Lang 1865, 9). The author was surely fooling nobody except possibly himself; in fact he was nearly as much a controversialist as was his fellow countryman John McLennan. Throughout his writing he not only quarreled with nearly all the other social evolutionary theorists, including occasionally McLennan; he also quarreled with Tylor and Frazer over their religious evolutionary schemes. He argued, on the basis of mythology, that belief in a benevolent creator-god was common among the most primitive peoples (Lang 1898). This seemingly approving estimate of "savage" thinking seems at odds with the contemptuous view of primitives that he elsewhere expressed. The difference between the controversialism of McLennan and that of Lang is largely a matter of style. McLennan's views are set out as dogmatic absolutes, those of Lang in drawn-out argumentation.

Lang's place in the history of anthropological thought is a modest one. As his biographer acknowledges, he was "in many ways a better critic than an original thinker [but he] performed a service for ethnology and the history of religions by examining current theories in the light of common sense and the ethnographic record (Lonergan 1991, 380). Among his critical contributions he surely does deserve credit for pointing out the fallacy of assuming that Australian culture was an evolutionary starting point, though this was not acknowledged by most of his fellows for a long time. His one truly original contribution was in adding totemism to the mix of anthropological thought and theory. However, on this subject he was soon overtaken by more profound and original thinkers.

It remains to add that totemism, as the supposed primeval form of religion, remained one of the hottest topics in anthropological discourse for about a generation. Like most intellectual fads, it came in time to be more and more widely and indiscriminately applied; for example, the mascots of college teams were identified by some as totems. However the topic lost much of its theoretical cogency when, after 1900, anthropology turned so largely away from evolutionary theory. Then, in 1910, Alexander Goldenweiser dealt the topic a nearly fatal blow with a lengthy and penetrating survey of the literature, in which he showed how nebulous the term totemism had become (Goldenweiser 1910).

CHAPTER EIGHT

W. ROBERTSON SMITH
AND ARAB MATRILINY

William Robertson Smith (1846-1894) was still another Scottish arm-chair anthropologist, and a disciple and friend of McLennan. His father was an ordained minister in the Free Church[8] of Scotland, and his son chose to follow the same path. His interests however were strictly schol-arly, not pastoral. He studied Semitic languages first at the University of Aberdeen and then at the Edinburgh Free College, where he received his ordination 1870. He then taught Oriental languages for a decade at the Free Church College of Aberdeen, and achieved a considerable scholarly reputation as a result of a number of articles especially in the *Encyclopaedia Britannica*. His liberal views however did not sit well with the rigidly Calvinist college authorities, and he was accused and tried for heresy. Though never formally convicted, or unfrocked, he was dismissed from his professorial post in 1881.

Smith was not out of work for long. He had been serving for some years as an assistant editor of the *Encyclopaedia Britannica,* and when the ailing editor-in-chief was forced to retire in 1881, Smith was chosen as his successor. He remained in that office until the 9th edition was completed in 1888. Meanwhile however he began an association with Cambridge University that was to continue for the rest of his life. He was appointed a professor of Arabic in 1883, became also the university

---

[8] i.e. free from state interference.

librarian in 1886, and in 1889 received the prestigious Sir Thomas Adams Professorship of Arabic, which he held until his death from tuberculosis four years later.

Major works

Perhaps due to the influence of his friend John McLennan, Robertson Smith was caught up in the surge of interest in early cultural evolution, and the search for cultural origins, that were prevalent at the end of the 19th century. That interest resulted in the two books for which he is chiefly remembered: *Kinship and Marriage in Early Arabia* in 1885 and *Lectures on the Religion of the Semites* in 1889.

Kinship and Marriage might be called "the quintessence of McLennanism" for the author accepted without reservation, at the outset, the tenets of his fellow Scotsman: that the earliest human societies were matrilineal, exogamous, and totemic. That being so, it must in the beginning have been true of Arab nomads as of all other peoples, even though their modern-day descendants appeared to be very much the opposite. Robertson Smith therefore drew on his unparalleled knowledge of early Arabic literature to try and find some supporting evidence for his views. But for all his scholarly endeavors, what he came up with is scanty and unconvincing. The argument for matriliny rests on arcane linguistic interpretations, having to do with the translation of early texts. Exogamy is taken as a given, because according to McLennan it always goes with matriliny. Totemism is demonstrated by the fact that a number of Semitic peoples worshipped animal gods.

In the end, Smith's argument really rests on a chain of presuppositions, linking back ultimately to the dogma of matrilineal priority: " . . . it is, I think, possible to shew that the Arabs had the system which McLennan has espoused under the name of totemism . . ., and if, as among other early nations, totemism and female kinship were combined with exogamy, it is also possible to construct, along the lines laid down in *Primitive Marriage,* a hypothetical picture of the social system, consistent with all the Arabian facts . . . ." (Smith 1885, xxi).

It seems strange today that Robertson Smith should have chosen Arab Bedouins, rather than Semitic peoples more generally, as the focus for his study. It was perhaps due to the fact that they, along with the Hebrews, are the only early Semitic peoples for whom kin-based social groups are clearly attested. It may also be however that the author accepted the erroneous belief, going all the way back to ancient Greek times, that pastoral nomadism represents a very early form of cultural adaptation, predating the earliest agriculture. We know today that it was in reality a specialized adaptation of the agricultural revolution, going back no more than 12,000 years.

Lectures on the Religion of the Semites represents Robertson Smith's attempt to reconstruct the ancestral religion common to all the Semitic peoples, on the basis of whatever can be learned about all the different Semitic-speaking groups. It involved the conviction that ritual, not belief, was the essential basis of the earliest religions: "the antique religions had for the most part no creed, they consisted entirely of institutions and practices" (Smith 1889, 16). For Semitic peoples, he argued, burnt sacrifice was the foremost of rituals, and represented a kind of communion. Here again however the author was the victim of scanty information as well as tortuous argumentation, and his effort was unconvincing.

Perspective

Kinship and Marriage is unique among the early contributions to the matriliny question in one respect: it is the only one that is at least partly inductive rather than deductive—based on evidence rather than pure logic. Moreover, it considerably widened the field of understanding on that issue. For those reasons the book in its time was widely read and respected, and went through several editions. Having a shaky empirical foundation, however, its importance was theoretical rather than factual, and it died along with the general belief in matrilineal priority. It is read today only as a landmark in the development of social anthropological thought.

The same may be said for *Religion of the Semites.* Its importance lies not in its substantive content but in the fact that it connected religion with social organization much more comprehensively than did totemic theory. As such it remains an important landmark in the field of sociology of religion, down to the present day.

CHAPTER NINE

C. N. STARCKE AND CULTURAL VARIABILITY

Carl Nicolai Starcke (1858-1926) was a well known and respected Danish politician, social philosopher, and author. He graduated from the University of Copenhagen 1883 with a thesis on political philosophy, and then immediately launched into a career as a liberal-to-radical politician and reformer. He was particularly interested in land reform and in pedagogical reform, and at one time helped to launch the first free high school in Europe. He had also a lifelong interest in family sociology, and in time published several books on the subject. Those works led in due course to his appointment as professor of philosophy at the University of Copenhagen, a position that he held until his death.

Starcke published altogether 15 books, variously in German and Danish, as well as one in French. I have been able to locate a translation only of the second of them, published in German as *Die primitive Familie und ihrer Entstehung und Entwicklung* in 1888, and translated into English in the following year as *The Primitive Family in its Origin and Development*. My comments here are based on an 1894 American edition.

The Primitive Family

This work represents nothing less than a radical intrusion into the kinship discourse; an intrusion of the Germanic empirical tradition in contrast to the Anglo-American philosophical tradition. Starcke was the first of the "kinship warriors" who had no evolutionary agenda. His aim was simply to reconstruct the earliest form or forms of human kinship organization, without reference to developmental sequences. To do so he would make use alike of ethnographic, historical, and mythic evidence.

Starcke was by no means the first student of kinship to draw on ethnographic data; Morgan and Tylor had already done so extensively. Those two scholars however were not true empiricists; they drew selectively on the ethnographic record to bolster their previously conceived theories. Starcke on the other hand followed the lead of the early German ethnographers, in amassing all the available data and then letting it speak for itself. As a result his work is far more factually comprehensive than is that of any predecessor. He was able to draw on the monumental German ethnographic encyclopedias that were published in the late 19th century—works that had no equivalent in any other language. (For extended discussion see Adams 1998, 286-96).

The result is that *The Primitive Family* is more nearly a cross-cultural survey than a theoretical essay. The chapters in Part I are arranged geographically, surveying available kinship data from Australia, America, Africa, Asia, and "Aryan" (i.e. Indo-European) peoples. In Part II the subject of kinship is taken up topically, with chapters on father and child, polyandry, the levirate, inheritance of wives, nomenclature, exogamy and endogamy, marriage, and extended kin groups.

From this exhaustively detailed survey the author came to two radical, and for many of his colleagues uncomfortable, conclusions. The first was that primitive systems of kinship were far more variable and unpredictable than anyone had supposed. The second was that, consequently, reconstructions of the evolution of kinship were futile. Variations could not be taken as survivals from different stages of evolutionary development, as all the previous commentators had supposed. "We can no more discover the first community than we can discover the first man; the history of mankind begins with a plurality of distinct groups, and hence the fact of a uniform beginning is at any rate doubtful" (Starcke 1894, 8). The existence of cultural plurality from the earliest times was almost the *leitmotiv* of the book.

Perspective

At least with respect to Anglo-American anthropology, Carl Starcke was a man ahead of his time. He anticipated by a generation the atheoretical objectivism of the Boasians. In some measure he anticipated, by two generations, the British functionalists when he asserted that, whatever their origins, kinship institutions must be understood as adaptations to existing circumstances. In small measure he even anticipated sociobiology in suggesting that the ultimate wellsprings of human social organization must be found in the animal kingdom (Starcke 1894, 8).

These are perhaps the reasons why *The Primitive Family* had little influence in its own time. The Anglo-Americans were simply not ready for it, for their largely conjectural speculations had yet to run their course. It was not until half a century later that Robert Lowie, from the same perspective as that of Starcke, rang down the curtain once and for all on the kinship wars.

CHAPTER TEN

C. STANILAND WAKE AND SEXUAL MORALITY

Charles Staniland Wake (1855-1910) is the ultimate forgotten man of Anglo-American anthropology—the only scholar discussed in this book who has no entry either in the *International Dictionary of Anthropologists* (Winters 1991) or in *Wikipedia*. His latter-day editor, Rodney Needham, has been able, through diligent search, to glean little more than the facts that he was born and educated in Kingston-on-Hull, England, and practiced law there until his unexplained emigration to America in 1889 or 1890. He settled in Chicago, where the city directory listed his profession as "journalist." He died in Chicago, with no known family or kinsmen, in 1910.

His published bibliography (Needham 1967, xliii-xlvi) shows that Wake had a lifelong interest in all things anthropological, and it is easy to guess that he took more interest in his avocation as anthropologist than in his vocation as lawyer, which he gave up even before he moved to America. In England he was involved in the rather convoluted internal politics of both of the Anthropological Institute (later the Royal Anthropological Institute) and the Ethnological Society, held offices in both societies, and then in 1873 founded the breakaway London Anthropological Society, which however failed after three years. After emigration he joined the American Antiquarian Society, wrote a number of articles for its journal, and in time became an associate editor. In 1895 he also joined the staff of the Field Columbian Museum (later the Field

Museum of Natural History), and in 1898 was appointed as a "preparator and clerk" in its Department of Anthropology (Needham 1967, ix-xii).

For the rest, Editor Needham writes

> None of Wake's papers can be found to have survived, the institutions for which he worked and the societies of which he was a member can tell nothing of him, and it has not even proved possible to find any portrait or other representation from which it might be learned what he looked like. In spite of the relative recency of his time, Wake is indeed a man who can be known only through his works. In these he shows himself to have been a man of very wide erudition, with a scholarly command of a variety of disparate subjects, and an unrelenting determination to further general enlightenment (Needham 1967, xiii).

Needham (1967, xii-xiv) goes on to suggest that Wake's obscurity may in part be a reflection of British class prejudice. He came from a bourgeois family in a smallish provincial town, did not attend a prestigious university, and throughout his life had no academic affiliation. Here also may perhaps be the explanation for his departure for the less class-ridden environment of Chicago.

The bibliography of Wake's known works includes 75 titles, the great majority of them anthropological. Articles relating to all four of anthropology's traditional subfields show that the author had a more comprehensive view of the discipline than had most of the evolutionary theorists of his time. There are in addition two articles on music, a book on the Egyptian Great Pyramid, a two-volume treatise on morality, and two privately printed volumes of rather idiosyncratic philosophy, which the author called "the geometry of science."

For all his obscurity, Staniland Wake has one absolutely unique distinction in the history of anthropology. He began his career as a British armchair anthropologist, and ended as an American ethnographer, thus bridging two disciplinary traditions that historically have had little interest in, or respect for, one another. (It may have been due to this apostasy that his British colleagues published no obituary notice at the time of Wake's death.) His early articles have broadly topical titles like "The Psychological Unity of Mankind," "Marriage by capture," and "Sacred Prostitution," typical of the armchair anthropology of the time. The American articles have titles like "The Navaho Origin Legend" and "Mythology of the Plains Indians," showing that the author had abandoned sweeping generalization and enlisted in the project of salvage ethnography among Native Americans, dominant in North American anthropology for half a century. It is intriguing to notice that Wake's years at the Field Columbian Museum coincided with the time when the young Franz Boas was designing the museum's Native American exhibits, and there is surely at least a possibility that it was Boas who inspired Wake's American studies. These were heavily concentrated in the fields of mythology and folklore—studies always of special interest to Boas.

The Development of Marriage and Kinship

This book is not Staniland Wake's only contribution to the kinship discourse, but it is the only one accessible today, thanks to its republication in a series called *Classics in Anthropology,* in 1967. The editor himself acknowledges that this is not really an apt characterization of the work, considering how little attention it received. Even Edward Westermarck, in his monumental *History of Human Marriage,* cites it only in a single footnote (Westermarck 1921, vol. 2, 193), and Radcliffe-Brown, in "The Study of Kinship Systems" (1941) ignores it completely. "It will be argued nevertheless that it is a work of classical merits, and it is on this account that it has been thought worthy of the labor of revival" says the editor (Needham 1967, vii).

Upon cursory reading, it is easy to see why the work may not have been popular. It is wordy to the point of prolixity, consisting mostly of endlessly drawn-out arguments against the work of others. Paragraphs two to three pages in length are filled with one ethnographic citation after another, all to support a single contention. The author has nevertheless a unique contribution to make, and it is set forth in his opening sentence: "Society is based on two instincts which are as powerful in their operation in the animal kingdom as with mankind—the instinct of self-preservation, and the sexual instinct" (Wake 1967, 1). Among all the commentators on kinship, Wake is the first to notice "the elephant in the room"—sex. All kinship systems have their origin in sexual activity, which is bound around with all kinds of attitudes and restrictions. Exogamy, for example, is not just a rule restricting kinship; it is a restriction on all sexual activity, which finds its reflection in kinship systems.

In contrast to earlier works in the kinship discourse, *The Development of Marriage and Kinship* is primarily about marriage, with limited attention given to the consanguinal aspects of kinship. Wake had strong personal values in regard to sex, which furnish the basis for his whole book. He was a sexual moralist, and so basically are all other humans, in his view. His reference is not necessarily to monogamous fidelity, but rather to the fact that people always a feel a compulsion to obey whatever are the rules of their particular society, because the existence of society itself depends on it. He had already published, twelve years earlier, a two-volume treatise to this effect (Wake 1878). Society may permit multiple wives or multiple husbands or situational sharing of mates, but there are always a great many kinds of couplings that are not permitted. Individuals often enough transgress, but they know that they are doing wrong. Thus there is, and always has been, some kind of recognized institution equivalent to marriage in all societies.

Therefore, he argues, there never was any such thing as the promiscuous horde, so dear to the imagination of McLennan, Morgan, and a good many others, and this is almost the whole focus of his book. The opening chapters are given over to refuting in rather tedious detail the arguments of McLennan, Morgan, Lubbock, and Bachofen, mostly by showing that they have misunderstood instances of permitted sexual license as being indicative of unlimited promiscuity. Three subsequent chapters discuss the marital rules and restriction found in societies that practice group marriage (two or more males in one group may cohabit with two or more females in another group, but with no one else), polyandry, polygyny, and monandry. In this extended survey the author again breaks fresh ground, by pointing out in detail the many different kinds of marital systems, preferences, and restrictions.

In late chapters, Wake turns to the reckoning of descent. Although he rejects out of hand the popular idea that matriliny was a necessary consequence of sexual promiscuity, he nevertheless believes that this was the preferred way of reckoning descent in most of the earliest societies. At the same time, he specifically denies that matrilineal descent implies matriarchal authority, as Bachofen had supposed (Wake 1967, 16). He has no convincing explanation for the precedence of matriliny, or for why so many societies later shifted to patrilineal reckoning, or for why some groups seem to have been patrilineal from the beginning. At times the author shows himself as an evolutionist, though he does not make it a major theme of his book: " . . . mankind has progressed upwards from a state of group-marriage, through polyandry and polygyny, to . . . monandry" (Wake 1967, 467). ("Monandry" refers to a marriage involving one and only one husband, but possibly more than one wife.)

In a penultimate chapter, the author attacks at length McLennan's theory of bride capture. The final chapter, on monogamy, identifies it as the culminating evolutionary stage because it is morally superior.

Perspective

I have to agree with Rodney Needham (1967, vii) that *The Development of Marriage and Kinship* deserves our attention not because it was influential but because it should have been. Who now can discuss kinship without reference to sex? Who can discuss marriage without recognizing the many kinds of marital systems and rules that exist? Yet the work can only be viewed as a milepost that was soon left behind. Two years after its appearance came Edward Westermarck's *History of Human Marriage* (1891), which covered all the same issues with greater clarity than Wake had done, and received the popular attention that never came to Staniland Wake.

CHAPTER ELEVEN

EDWARD WESTERMARCK AND THE SOCIOLOGY OF SEX

Edvard Alexander Westermarck (1862-1939), as he was originally christened, was a Finnish Swede, born in Helsinki and educated at its university. After graduation he taught at the University of Helsinki for 15
years. During and after those years he published a considerable number
of articles in Finnish, but all his major books from the beginning were
published in English. Two of them, *The History of Human Marriage*
(1891) and *The Origin and Development of the Moral Ideas* (1906-1908)
attracted wide attention and led to the author's appointment as the first
professor of sociology at the London School of Economics, which thereafter remained his main institutional home. There he became one of the
founders of British social anthropology and the teacher of Bronislaw
Malinowski, among many others. His interests from the beginning extended far beyond the then recognized limits of anthropology, and he is
regularly labeled in works of reference as a sociologist and philosopher
as well as an anthropologist.

Westermarck was the first of the kinship theorists who was also a
bona fide ethnographer in the modern sense. He undertook four years of
fieldwork in Morocco, in search of the cross-cultural insights that would
inform his works on human morality. They resulted also in several purely
ethnographic works, including *Ritual and Belief in Morocco* (1926a) and
Wit and Wisdom in Morocco (1930). His fieldwork however was carried

out subsequent to the original publication of *The History of Human Marriage,* which relied for ethnography entirely on literary sources.

The History of Human Marriage

Edward Westermarck was every bit as much a moralist as was Staniland Wake, and like Wake he also published a multi-volume work on morality in general (1906-8), in addition to his work specifically on marriage and kinship. He undertook to write on these latter subjects for precisely the same reason as did Wake (of whose work he was unaware at the time): he wanted to explode the idea of the promiscuous horde. His chapters on that subject (Chapters IV-VI) are generally similar to those of Wake, as he marshals a wide variety of evidence against the promiscuity theory. Thereafter however he strikes out in quite different directions. His book, as the title suggests, is almost entirely about marriage rather than kinship more broadly, as he explores in great detail the origins of marriage, factors affecting the choice of mates, courtship customs, exogamy and endogamy, means of mate acquisition, and the many forms of marriage.

Although history is brought into the discussion from time to time, it is not really the main theme of the work, which is more nearly a cross-cultural survey. Notably lacking is the evolutionary scenario dominant in nearly all earlier works. On the contrary, the author demonstrated that the distribution of different forms of marriage among different peoples is so inconsistent and irregular that they cannot be fitted into any neat evolutionary sequence. Unlike Wake, he saw clearly that destruction of the promiscuity hypotheses left no logical reason for believing in the priority of matrilineal descent. The oldest and most basic form of the family, he decided, was the same that prevails today in most of the world: the father-headed nuclear family.

Almost from the moment of its publication, *The History of Human Marriage* achieved the success that had eluded Staniland Wake. Within thirty years it had undergone five editions, as more and more ethnographic detail was added; the last edition (1921) encompassed three volumes. At that point the author recognized the need for a shorter version, which was achieved with *A Short History of Human Marriage* (1926b). The book is not just a condensation; it includes two entirely new chapters, "Consent as a Consideration of Marriage" and "Marriage by Consideration and the Exchange of Presents" which are based in part on the author's Moroccan researches. Omitted altogether are the three chapters attacking the doctrine of primitive promiscuity—the original reason for writing the book—for that battle was over, and Westermarck had won.

Westermarck is remembered above all for his theory of the incest tabu: " . . . there is a remarkable absence of erotic feelings between persons living very close together since childhood. . . .as in many other cases, sexual indifference is combined with the positive feeling of aversion . . ." (Westermarck 1926b, 80). Among social theorists this has been known ever since as the "Westermarck principle."

Perspective

In his sweeping overview of all the different factors involved in marriage, and his abundant citation of ethnographic sources, Westermarck was far ahead of any other commentator on the subject. In that sense, *The History of Human Marriage* is at least as important as a work of sociology as of anthropology. Yet for all the plethora of his sources, Westermarck was not a true empiricist; like nearly all the kinship theorists he was prone to "cherry-pick" his data to fit his theories (cf. especially Lowie 1937, 97-9). The best that can be said is that, with so much actual data at his command, he was less given to dogmatism than were his predecessors.

At the same time, by concentrating almost entirely on marriage, Westermarck had sidestepped some of the most contentious issues of the kinship wars, relating to the roles of kinship nomenclature, totemism, and the like. *The History of Human Marriage* was criticized by the likes of Lang, Robertson Smith, and Durkheim in considerable part because of the issues it did not take up. At any rate it did not by any means put an end to the kinship wars, as will be evident from the succeeding paragraphs.

CHAPTER TWELVE

JOSEF KOHLER, COMPREHENSIVE CRITIC

Josef Kohler (1849-1919), a Professor of Law at the University of Berlin, was yet another learned jurist who felt compelled to have his say in the kinship debate. Like most of the other jurists he was a teacher rather than a practicing barrister, first at the University of Wurzberg and later at Humboldt University in Berlin. He became in time a world authority both on the history and the philosophy of law. His other major interests were in ethnography and in art history, and he published also a good deal of poetry. His works are remarkable above all for their erudition, for he traveled widely and read incessantly in at least half a dozen languages; something that is very evident in all his publications.

Although several of the early kinship theorists, including the four earliest ones, were jurists, Kohler was the first who had actually made a study of both tribal and peasant law, as represented in ethnographic literature. Over a period of a decade he published articles on the traditional law of the Australians, the Chinese, the Malayans, several different provinces of India, Ceylon, the Eskimo, and early Americans, in the *Zeitschrift für vergleichende Rechtswissenschaft (Journal for the Comparative Study of Law)*, of which he was editor. Much of this material in time provided the basis for *On the Prehistory of Marriage*, originally published in German in 1897.

Kohler, in the spirit of his times, was philosophically an evolutionist. "A spirit of unity rules mankind, and evolution forces its way out of universal substance," he wrote in the preface to his *Philosophy of Law* (1921, xliv). However, he saw the course of evolution as frequently erratic and unpredictable; he wrote that " . . . even if progress appears certain, yet the way is altogether uncertain" (Ibid., 21).

On the Prehistory of Marriage

This curious volume is nearly unintelligible until the reader becomes aware that the author has made two major conceptual errors, while the translators have added still another.

First, Kohler has simply equated clan organization with totemism as if they were opposite sides of the same coin. At times he actually uses the terms "clan" and "totem" interchangeably, ignoring the fact that one designates a system of social organization, the other a system of religious belief. Insofar as they can be separated, Kohler actually believes that totemism came first, as when he writes "The totem belief is one of humanity's civilizing and vigorous religious impulses, for it contains the seed of the future structure of the family and state" (Kohler 1975, 105). In fact totemism cannot exist except in reference to particular groups; it could not exist in advance of them. And if totemism by definition is found only in societies with clan organization or its equivalent, it does not at all follow, as the author assumes, that all clans are totemic. Contrary to Kohler's specific assertion (1975, 105-12), the majority of North American Indian clans are not.

Second, the author assumes *apriori* that the seven different systems of kinship nomenclature designated by Morgan in *Systems of Consanguinity* (1871) are indicative of basically different systems of organization. Peoples having the Crow system are said to be necessarily matrilineal; those with the Omaha system are necessarily patrilineal (1975, 57-68). This in fact is not universally true, but more importantly the whole issue of whether or not kinship nomenclature correlates with social organization remains controversial to this day. Luminaries such as A. L. Kroeber and Leslie Spier have insisted that kinship terms imply nothing about either belief or behavior (Spier 1925).

The translators have further muddied the waters by translating *Mutterrecht* as "Mother-Right" (as also have the translators of Bachofen). *Recht* in German means primarily law or rule rather than entitlement, and *Mutterrecht* is no more than the standard German term for matrilineal reckoning, coined or at least popularized by Bachofen. No specific entitlements are implied—certainly not matriarchy.

The English edition consulted here opens with a very long Editor's Introduction (Barnes 1975). The earlier pages are extremely useful in contextualizing the work, recapitulating the development of the kinship debate up the time of its publication. The later pages have no relevance to Kohler's work; they are given over to the kind of nitpicking, "what goes with what" that has been typical of the kinship discourse since matrilineal descent, totemism, and group marriage have ceased to be significant issues for all but a few specialists.

Turning to Kohler's work itself, titled in the original *Zur Urgeschichte der Ehe* (1897), it was one of the author's last major works, coming on the heels of years of ethnographic reading and publishing on the law of particular peoples. It consists essentially of three stand-alone essays that first appeared separately in the *Zeitschrift für vergleichende Rechtswissenschaft,* then were brought together in book form in the same year.

The first essay is simply and aptly titled "Critique." It is aimed at critics, named and unnamed, who have attacked the work of Lewis Henry Morgan. This is an essential preface to the remainder of the work, for the third essay is based in its entirety on Morgan's kinship tables. Singled out for criticism in particular are Westermarck, for his *History of Human Marriage,* and an obscure German author, Johann Richard Mucke, the title of whose book would translate in English as "Horde and Family in their Earliest Development: a New Theory Based on Statistics" (1895). (In fact it has never been translated.) Kohler's arguments are somewhat convoluted, but they add up to the fact that the authors in question have failed to prove their case. Kohler was every bit as much a controversialist as were McLennan or Lang, and his criticisms are often stated in comparably acerbic terms.

The second essay has the title "Totemism and Mother-Right." Here Kohler repeats essentially the same error as in the case of totemism and clans. Having assumed that totemism and clans are inseparably linked, he now shows that matrilineal descent is found almost entirely in clan or lineage-organized societies. Therefore it follows, he suggests, that totemism and matrilinealism are also inseparably linked. This had already been suggested by McLennan, but Kohler goes on suggest for the first time that totemism naturally leads to polygyny, an idea that is further developed in the third essay.

The final essay, which is very much the focal point of the work, has the title "Group Marriage among the American Indians, Australians, and Dravidians." "Group marriage" here does not mean a single marital unit involving *both* multiple husbands and multiple wives, although this is a theoretical possibility according to Kohler's reckoning. It is here just an umbrella terms for all forms of polygyny and polyandry.

The chapter is based almost in its entirety on the kinship tables in Morgan's *Systems of Consanguinity and Affinity* (1871), and no fewer than 61 of them are reproduced by Kohler. His basic assumption is that a man may always marry any of the females in the system that are called by the same term as mother, and a woman may always marry any of the males that are called by the same term as father. This is shown to be a possibility in every one of the diagrams presented. They serve to illustrate, *ad infinitum,* the different combinations than may occur in polygynous families, depending on who is and is not called "mother" or "father" in a particular system. ("Mother" for example will nearly always include also her sister, but may or may not include also her daughter by a previous marriage, her parallel cousin, her aunt, or even more distant cognates of the same clan.) Only in the latter pages of the essay does the author turn from possibilities to actualities, citing cases where polygyny or, very rarely, polyandry had actually been reported.

The author's two-page Conclusion offers a classic example of being right for the wrong reasons:

> That all the peoples of the earth originally had group
> marriages appears irrefutable if we consider the follow-
> ing points: (1) the connection between group marriage
> and totemism, and how the one derives from the other;

(2) how these not at all closely connected peoples developed matching group-marriage systems with only
individual variations and characteristic features; (3) that
these are peoples whose totemism [read kinship system]
indicates a special originality for their culture; (4) that
totemism [read kinship organization] presents itself in
nearly all human activities, legends, idioms, as an ancient and later abandoned system (Kohler 1975, 233).

Perspective

In taking Morgan's kinship tables as his starting point, and treating
them as behavioral actualities, Kohler has offered us a quintessential
example of mistaking pigeonholes for pigeons; of equating possibility
with actuality. He delineates an enormous number of possible family
structures, with no indication at all as to how often if ever they actually
occurred. He has also shown that different relatives are permitted or
forbidden as marriage partners in different kinship schemes, with no
explanation why this is so except that it is prescribed by their names.

In the end this author has done little more than to demonstrate what
few anthropologists have ever doubted: that a requirement of monogamy
was rare if not non-existent in tribal society. Within any system, support must be guaranteed for everyone, and in situations where males or
(much more rarely) females are scarce, what more obvious solution than
through plural marriages? But the fact that it was always possible is no
indication of how often it actually happened. When in 1954 I studied
the Navajo community of Shonto, where polygyny was traditionally
permitted, I found that only 8% of marriages were actually polygynous
(Adams 1963, 63).

Koher's volume, like Staniland Wake's *Development of Marriage and
Kinship*, has been selected for inclusion in the Chicago series of Classics
in Anthropology, which seems to have provided the occasion for its
translation into English. Nevertheless, designation as a "classic" seems
even more dubious here than in the case of Wake. By the time of this

translation, in 1975, matriliny, totemism, and polygyny had long since ceased to be absorbing issues, and I have in fact never seen a reference to this book in any other anthropological work. Perhaps it had a wider audience in Germany, where its author was famous for his other writings.

CHAPTER THIRTEEN

ERNEST CRAWLEY
AND SEXUAL TABU

Alfred Ernest Crawley (1869-1924) was very much a maverick among the kinship theorists. By inclination he was first and foremost a sports-man—a winner of several tennis trophies, quarter-finalist at Wimbledon, and the author of a number of popular books on sport. He came by it honestly, for his father, a clergyman, was also keen on sports, and his brother was an Olympic tennis champion. Although tennis was his favorite sport, Ernest also excelled at golf, figure-skating, and shooting.

Crawley studied classics at Cambridge, and thereafter taught the subject at a succession of boys' schools, eventually becoming headmaster of one. Two years later however he abruptly turned his back on the educational scene to devote himself entirely to sports and to writing. He wrote several books and a long succession of articles about sports, mainly lawn tennis.

According to a *Wikipedia* article, Crawley at some unspecified point was ordained a minister, but resigned from the church in 1913 under terms of the Clerical Disabilities Act. However, his outlook throughout his life remained decidedly clerical. In addition to sports he wrote a number of books and articles on the history of religion, and it may have been these that led in turn to the study of primitive culture. This in turn, he tells us, led him more specifically to the study of primitive marriage (Crawley 1927, x). In time it would lead to his only well-known book:

The Mystic Rose, a Study of Primitive Marriage and of Primitive Thought in its Bearing on Marriage (1902).

The Mystic Rose[9]

This book was first published, in two volumes, fairly early in Crawley's career (1902); indeed, before he had turned his main interest to sports. Twenty-two years later he was persuaded to prepare an extensive revision, but died unexpectedly before he had made more than a beginning. The task was taken up and finished by his friend and fellow writer Theodore Besterman, who added a lot of new ethnographic material as well as some discussion, and refutation of some of Crawley's critics (Crawley 1927). The discussion here is based on the 1927 edition, which combines the original two volumes under one cover but retains their separate pagination. The subtitle of the book is somewhat misleading, for it is really about the psychology of sex in general. Marriage in the usual sense comes in for discussion only near the end of the work.

Crawley's clerical background is clearly evident throughout his book, for its underlying theme is right out of Genesis: sex is polluting, and women are to blame. Therefore, runs the argument, women are dangerous because sex is dangerous. Women must be brought under control because sex must be brought under control. As is evident here, the author often treats the words "women" and "sex" as though they were synonymous. While a kind of folk wisdom holds that in the beginning women invented marriage in order to bring men under control, Crawley turns the thesis on its head: men invented marriage in order to bring women under control.

The empirical basis for the work, such as it is, consists mainly of the sexual tabus which are found in every society, and which the author equates with tabus on women. All of them, in his view, derive from the belief that sex must be limited because it is polluting. His early chapters, collectively titled "The Taboo Imposed," seek to explain how and why women came to be regarded as inferior and dangerous. Later chapters,

---

[9] The title is nowhere fully explained, but Mystic Rose is one of the appellations given to the Virgin in Roman Catholic Mariology.

with the collective title "The Taboo Removed," tell how prejudice against women was mitigated through a variety of social controls and rituals, but above all through marriage. In Volume 2, under the heading "Secondary Taboo," the author shows how the pollution tabu is reimposed to regulate the relations between husbands and wives, between marriage partners and their affines, and between parents and children. The arguments in each of the chapters are supported by a plethora of ethnographic examples.

Although Crawley, like nearly all the anthropologists of his time, was much concerned with cultural origins, his book does not directly address the issue in the case of marriage. He gives an abundsnce of arguments to show *why* the institution came into being, but not how, when, or where it happened. The basis of his argument is thus functional rather than genuinely historical, and from that perspective all the ethnographic examples are beside the point.

Perspective

Staniland Wake was the first to introduce sex as a serious factor in the kinship discourse, and Westermarck made it a major theme in *A History of Human Marriage*. Crawley however went a long step further in introducing, for the first time, the psychology of sex. This at the time was decidedly novel, and attained for the work a considerable readership. Westermarck is quoted as calling it " . . . . one of the most important books on social anthropology ever published. My own writings . . . give ample evidence of my great indebtedness to it." To Malinowski it was " . . . a work which appears to me among the best and most important of the psychological studies in primitive custom" (both quotations are from the dust jacket of the book.)

Crawley in fact had no psychological training, and the psychology in *The Mystic Rose* is essentially "pop psychology." Like all the other early kinship theorists who had never been near a tribesman, Crawley offers sweeping generalizations about "savage" culture, and about the childlike simplicity of the "savage" mind, as though these were demonstrated facts. In addition to this, however, he is unique in also attributing to the "savage" mind what was in fact the misogynistic outlook of his own time and class, as though this was a human universal. Though ultimately rooted in the Book of Genesis, it reflected at least as strongly the "masculist" British culture of the late Victorian and Edwardian eras. This was a world of elite boys' schools where the youngsters were taught Spartan self-discipline; of all-male universities; of gentlemen's clubs where no woman dared set foot; and of popular adventure novels which celebrated the virtues and the achievements of manliness. In this world of imagination women were an unwelcome intrusion and a debilitating, not to say polluting, force, standing between a man and the full realization of his manhood. Amateur sports, Crawley's lifelong passion, were very much a part of the picture.

Notwithstanding the early accolades of Westermarck and Malinowski, *The Mystic Rose* found no lasting place in the anthropological literature. Its main appeal was very probably to Crawley's own "masculist" set. At any rate I have never seen the book cited in any serious anthropological work later than its own time. For later anthropologists it might still be useful as a minutely detailed catalogue of sexual tabus and customs, but it is fatally flawed by ethnocentrism; by imputing to the primitive mind the cultural prejudices of its own time and religion. All peoples have indeed always recognized that sex is powerful and therefore dangerous, but equating power and danger with impurity is a distinctly Abrahamic (i.e. Judaeo-Christian-Muslim) conception. To other peoples, the idea that humans were not meant by the gods to have sex is the ultimate absurdity.

CHAPTER FOURTEEN

ERNEST SIDNEY HARTLAND: BACK TO BACHOFEN

Edwin Sidney Hartland (1848-1927) was yet one more jurist who felt the urge to plunge into the kinship waters. Unlike most of his predecessors he was a practicing solicitor rather than a teacher. He was born in the London suburb of Islington, where his father was a Congregationalist minister, but practiced law mainly in the Welsh city of Swansea.

Hartland's anthropological interests were above all in mythology and folklore, and he served at one time as president of the Folklore Society. However he also wrote a number of works on kinship, including a two-volume study on *Primitive Paternity* (1909). That he was not an anthropologist in the modern sense (and possibly also that he was the son of a minister) is made clear by his disdain for the very tribal peoples who were his subjects. Arunta performances are "obscene" (Hartland 1921, 20); The Fuegians are "perhaps the lowest and most miserable of all" (Ibid., 25).

The Primitive Family

This quaint little volume, published in 1921, takes us right back to Bachofen. Its sole purpose, clearly stated at the outset, is to uphold the doctrine of matrilineal priority against its critics (Hartland 1921, 2). The author however, unlike a number of predecessors, was not a controversialist. With very rare exceptions, he argued his case not by attacking the critics of matrilineal theory but simply by documenting the frequency of matrilineal descent systems, all over the world. His book seems to be a popularization of an earlier treatise on the subject that he had published as a Memoir of the American Anthropological Association (1917).

Chapter I reviews a few of the early works on kinship theory. Chapter II, "The Beginnings of Society," restates the old argument about uncertain paternity in early society, providing the essential reason for matriliny. In Chapter III, "Rudimentary Forms," he describes the apparent absence of any semblance of government among certain peoples who at the time were considered to be the most primitive: Tierra del Fuegians, Andaman Islanders, Tasmanians, and Eskimos.

Chapter IV, "Mother-Right, its Characteristics," enumerates what the author believes to be the characteristics of matrilineal societies, including matrilocal residence, clan organization, female clan heads, and inheritance of male property from maternal uncle to nephew. The next seven chapters are devoted to discussion of matrilineal societies as they have been reported from Australia (Chapter V), Oceania (Chapter VI), Africa (Chapter VII), India (Chapter VIII), Indonesia (Chapter IX), Asia, the Mediterranean Basin, and Europe (Chapter X), and America (Chapter XI). The concluding Summary (Chapter XII) recapitulates the author's arguments.

Perspective

Kinship theory was born out of logic, not ethnographic reality, and this volume illustrates how strongly the logical factor persisted in spite of the ever-increasing weight of ethnography. The idea of primeval promiscuity fitted nicely with the Victorian conception of primeval society, whose institutions were presumed to be just the opposite of whatever was modern. As long as one accepted that premise, the logic of matrilineal priority was unimpeachable. But once it was shown that no such condition of unrestrained promiscuity ever existed, the logical support for matrilineal priority vanished. Hartland was forced instead to argue his

case by cataloguing the very large number of matrilineal societies that
had been documented, ignoring the fact that frequency does not demonstrate priority. He did at times recognize the existence of patriliny among
some fairly primitive tribes, but suggested, without much evidence, that
it had succeeded an original matrilineal system.

CHAPTER FIFTEEN

W. H. R. RIVERS: A WIDENING VISION

The work of William Halse Rivers Rivers[10] (1864-1922) marks a major turning point in kinship studies, for he was the first of all the learned theorists who had seen genuinely primitive tribesmen, both in India and in Melanesia, and whose ideas about kinship were significantly influenced thereby. He was the very antithesis of the armchair scholar, having been by turns a ship's surgeon, an ethnographic researcher, a wartime army doctor, and an experimental psychologist.

Rivers came from a comfortable but not wealthy middle-class family in the London suburbs; his father was a speech therapist. (Ironically, his son suffered all his life from a stammer.) He went to good private schools and was destined for Cambridge, but was prevented from enrolling by a bout of typhoid fever. After recovery he decided instead to study medicine at the University of London, where he received his M.D. in 1888. He then sought to enlist as an army surgeon, but was turned down again because of the typhoid. Instead, he found employment as a ship's surgeon, and made a number of voyages, including to North America and Japan. Then, in 1887, came the first of a series of appointments as house surgeon in a succession of London hospitals, and he began simultaneously to study psychology and neurology. Increasingly, he turned his

---

[10] There is no clear explanation for the second "Rivers," which may have been due to a clerical error on his birth registry.

interest toward abnormal psychology and mental disease. As a result, in 1893 he was offered a lectureship in psychology at Cambridge. In 1904, he founded and subsequently edited the *British Journal of Psychology*.

It was because of his psychological expertise that Rivers was recruited by A. C. Haddon to join the famous Cambridge Torres Straits Expedition in 1898. His task was specifically to run various tests on the mentality and perceptions of the Melanesian islanders. The experience was not especially productive for Rivers, but it did awaken in him a life-long secondary interest in ethnology. Two years later he went on another field expedition to administer perception tests on Egyptians. Then, in 1901-2, he undertook by himself a six-month study of the Toda hill tribe of India, which resulted in a classic monograph (Rivers 1906). In 1907-8 and again in 1914-15 he did further field survey work in Melanesia, resulting in the two-volume *History of Melanesian Society* (1914a).

When Rivers returned from the field, World War I had begun, and he contributed his services by enlisting as surgeon at a military hospital, specializing in psychological problems. He gained considerable notice for his successful treatment of a number of cases that were then known as "shell-shock" (now "post-traumatic stress disorder"). Among his patients, who became fixed friends, were the poets Siegfried Sassoon and Robert Graves. After the war he continued at Cambridge to teach, to conduct research, and to write on psychology, but at the same time he became more and more absorbed in the "kinship game." In his posthumously published memoir, *Conflicts and Dreams* (1923), he confessed that the claims of ethnology were so insistent as to have decided him to abandon work in physiology, medicine, and psychology, in each of which he had achieved considerable success (paraphrased in Elliot Smith 1926, v). He served as president of the [British] Folk-Lore Society in 1921-22, and was elected president of the Royal Anthropological Institute in 1922, but died before he could complete his term. His final work in ethnology was *Social Organization,* published posthumously in 1923.

Social organization

This book is based on a manuscript which Rivers prepared in 1920, but had intended extensively to revise. Following his death the task was taken on instead by W. J. Perry. The work is based on a series of lectures, and Perry found it in a very incomplete and somewhat disordered state, requiring a substantial amount of revision and reorganization. The lectures must have been intended for an elementary audience, for the author devotes considerable time to defining terms and explaining concepts that by this time were in common circulation among anthropologists. How the book relates to his earlier work, *Kinship and Social Organization*, published in 1914, I do not know, for I have not seen the earlier work.

Social Organization is for all practical purposes an elementary textbook. The initial chapters discuss the categories of organization that were by now familiar to all anthropologists: The Family; Clan, moiety, and tribe; Marriage; Kinship and relationships, Father-right and mother-right. The general thrust in these as well as later chapters is to suggest that things were not so simple as the armchair evolutionists had supposed. The chapter on Kinship and relationships makes the point that classificatory (that is, extended) systems are not mere matters of nomenclature; they embed important information about the nature of society. This is argued in great detail, though the author really demonstrates only that kinship terms serve to delimit marriage choices. Nevertheless it became, a generation later, basic dogma to British social anthropologists.

The chapter on Father-right and mother-right states unequivocally that no case can be made for the priority of either system. It also makes an important and long-overdue observation: that descent, patrilineal or matrilineal, may or may not determine inheritance of property, succession to office, exercise of authority, or place of residence. (Among the matrilineal Navajos, the people best known to me, it determines none of those things.) In short, descent is often not nearly as important a social determinant as earlier theorists had supposed. To the extent that this assertion was accepted, it served to take some of the cogency out of the kinship debate.

Among later chapters, that on Property rediscovers, among primitive societies, the corporate kin group long ago recognized by Maine.

The chapter on Fraternities and secret societies importantly shows that there was more to primitive society than kinship, though this point had already been made by Lowie a few years earlier (1920). The chapter on Occupation, class and caste recognizes that social stratification is not uncommon in the tribal world, and is most often based on occupation. The chapter on Government makes the interesting point that authority in the Old World regularly rests on a religious sanction, whereas in aboriginal America there were purely secular chiefs who ruled by election.

Of the three appendices, the first two are both meant to show that kinship organization was a much more complex matter than Morgan had supposed. The third, inserted by Perry, stresses the prevalence of dual (i.e. moiety) organization in many societies, and suggests that it was a feature of the earliest societies.

Perspective

Robert Lowie writes of Rivers that his sociological researches " . . . must not be judged by the posthumously published work on that subject [i. e. *Social Organization*], based as it was on meager lecture notes, but by sundry special essays. Rivers veritably revived the sociological study of kinship terms, which had virtually ceased through revulsion at some of the rasher of Morgan's theses" (Lowie 1937, 171). However, Lowie's somewhat disparaging view of *Social Organization* may be colored by the fact that four years earlier his own *Primitive Society* (1920) had covered much the same ground.

Be that as it may, *Social Organization* when published was highly valuable as a comprehensive overview of the state of social anthropology at the time. And it had then, and has now, a more specific virtue, stemming from the author's extensive fieldwork. It shows in great detail that the whole field of kinship is very much more complex, and less predictable, than previous discussants had supposed. Rivers' book differs from that of Lowie especially in that it assigns far more importance specifically to kinship terminology, and consequently devotes far more space to it.

Rivers was not a controversialist. Although his ideas were often stated very forcefully, including his criticism of earlier theories, they were never offered in a spirit of confrontation. It should also be noted that *Social Organization* was published at a time when the kinship wars had largely run their course. The work as a result did not generate as much heat, or ever as much attention. as it would have a generation earlier.

CHAPTER SIXTEEN

ROBERT H. LOWIE:
THE FINAL SALVO

Robert Harry Lowie (1883-1957) was born in Vienna and spent his first ten years there. But despite his lifelong attachment to all things German, it is surprising to find that he has told us nothing at all about his Austrian boyhood. The second paragraph of his autobiography finds him already in high school in New York (Lowie 1959, 1). His father, we learn from other sources (Murphy 1972, 9) was a not very successful businessman.

The Lowie family came to New York in 1893, along with the flood of other German-speaking immigrants who arrived in those years. They were so numerous that New York City for a time was said to be the third largest German-speaking community in the world. It was known to its inhabitants as *Kleindeutschland* (Little Germany), and had its own German-language schools, newspapers, clubs, and theaters. Its ambience had a powerful influence on the young Lowie, suffused as it was with the humanistic liberalism of Kantian (i.e. German Idealist) philosophy (cf. especially Adams 1998, 269-334).

The Lowie family, like many of the German immigrants, were Jewish, but like many also it was something they wanted to leave behind. Lowie in his autobiography never identifies himself as Jewish, and makes only brief, passing reference to having Jewish relatives.

Like nearly all middle-class Germans, the Lowie family venerated higher education as an end in itself—it was the mark of a gentleman. Though family finances were limited, Lowie enrolled for undergraduate study at City College of New York, then went for graduate study to Columbia University. His intentional intention was to study psychology, but in due course he encountered the charismatic Franz Boas and anthropology, and became an instant convert to both. He received his PhD in anthropology in 1908, and was in fact the first of the "kinship warriors" to hold that degree. His dissertation dealt with a particular, recurring theme in North American Indian mythology.

Boas and nearly all his students, including Lowie, regarded anthropology as first and foremost a field discipline—a branch of natural history. They had set themselves a primary task of recording for posterity as much as could be salvaged from the disappearing cultures and languages of Native Americans, and this became Lowie's nearly exclusive concern during his earliest professional years. He worked for more than a decade as a research assistant at the American Museum of Natural History in New York, with a primary responsibility for collecting Native American ethnographic materials and data. In due time he carried out field studies among at least a dozen different tribes—possibly the largest number ever studied in the field by any one ethnographer. His special favorites were the Crow Indians of Montana, whom he visited many times, and on whom he became an acknowledged expert. His monograph *The Crow Indians* (Lowie 1935) is still regarded as one of the classics of American ethnography.

In 1921 Lowie was offered a position as professor of anthropology at the University of California (Berkeley), which he occupied until his retirement in 1950. Thereafter he did little more fieldwork, but gained an increasing and eventually worldwide reputation for his writings on ethnological theory, with emphasis especially on social organization. He read voraciously, and his encyclopedic knowledge in time became legendary. Along with a host of articles he published two seminal books, *Primitive Society* in 1920 and *Social Organization* in 1948.

Primitive Society

This is Lowie's attempt to bring a properly critical perspective to the topics of social organization in general, and kinship in particular, which for so long had been the subject of highly imaginative and at times far-fetched theorizing. The book is a wide-ranging survey—the first of its kind—over the whole field of primitive society. Kinship in the narrower sense is not given special attention; the author in fact devotes a great deal more discussion to the clan, or the sib as he prefers to call it.

The first eight chapters range over the long-familiar topics of marriage, polygamy, the family, kinship usages, the sib [clan], history of the sib, and the position of women. He treats each in a strictly down-to-earth, "just the facts" manner, to suggest how much we really can and (especially) cannot generalize about each. Subsequent chapters deal similarly with property, associations, theory of associations, rank, government, and justice. Through all of them, Lowie exhibits his unrivaled command of worldwide ethnographic literature; he arrives at his basic conclusion, that you can't generalize about primitive society, only after a review of masses of data.

The two chapters on associations are the most novel in the book, demonstrating that there was more to primitive society than kinship. Lowie was the first to recognize the importance of non-kin based groupings in the social scheme. He goes on to discuss the many different kinds of associations that are recorded in ethnographic literature: medicine societies, hunting societies, warrior societies, dancing societies, clown societies, and women's societies, among others.

The chapter on the position of women likewise breaks fresh ground, discussing their actual functions in society rather than seeing them merely as pawns (or queens) in the kinship game. In typically Lowian fashion he speaks of the " . . . great caution required in summing up the status of the female sex in a given society. The conditions involved in the relations of men and women are many-sided and it is dangerous to overweight one particular phase of them. *Least of all should excessive significance be attached to theory*" [italics inserted] (Lowie 1920, 188). Like most of the works of Lowie, *Primitive Society* is first and foremost a worldwide ethnographic survey, with conclusions secondary. Indeed when it was published, many reviewers decried its atheoretical and at times antitheoretical stance.

After publication of *Primitive Society,* Lowie ran across an older book, *Der Staat,* by Fritz Oppenheimer (1907), and was led to recognize that his own book had given insufficient attention to the topic of government. Accordingly, in 1927 he published what amounts to a brief addendum, in another book (originally an article) with the title *The Origin of the State.* His most important point was that warfare (ignored by all the earlier theorists) is common in primitive societies, and may have an important influence on social organization. It may lead both to social stratification and to territoriality.

Social Organization

Significant changes overtook American anthropology in the years after World War I. Put in the simplest terms, it shifted its main focus from the past to the present, and ceased to be primarily a historical discipline. Indians remained for the moment the main focus of study, but instead of recovering vanished culture from the memory of old men and women, ethnographers now studied the ongoing situation on the reservations. As a result anthropology for the first time became susceptible to outside influences, particularly from psychology and from economics. Moreover, a certain number of Americans were now doing fieldwork in Latin America, and a few in Africa. As a result, Lowie came to recognize that *Primitive Society* was due for a considerable overhaul, including dropping *Primitive* from the title. The result was *Social Organization,* published in 1948.

The work is nevertheless recognizably a remake of *Primitive Society,* covering all the original topics as well as a couple of new ones, and generally retaining the original organization. The book now concludes with four illustrative case studies of "social organization in action," encompassing the Crow Indians of Montana, the Buinese of Melanesia, the Shilluk of central Africa, and imperial Austria. The book however will not be further discussed in these pages, because by 1948 the kinship wars were long in the past, thanks in considerable part to the work of Lowie himself.

Perspective

Lowie's work, in its quietly revolutionary way, must be seen as part of a much more general anthropological revolution, on both sides of the Atlantic. In America it was led by Franz Boas and his students; in England by Bronislaw Malinowski, A. R. Radcliffe-Brown and their students. Both groups turned their backs completely on the purely speculative social evolutionary theories, and the search for cultural origins, that had preoccupied their predecessors. The Boasians turned instead to studying the cultural development of particular peoples or cultures, the Malinowskians to analyzing culture from the perspective of its functions. On both sides of the Atlantic, these developments signaled the end of the kinship wars. Decoupled from evolutionary theory, kinship studies continued to be interesting, but they were no longer important. All the heat was gone.

Although the kinship wars were in the broadest sense a victim of their times, the part played by Lowie in bringing about their demise should not be overlooked. While most of his fellows were simply ignoring the simplistic armchair theorists of yesteryear, Lowie chose to contend with them. Throughout his books, in one domain of culture after another, he matter-of-factly and with great erudition demonstrated that all the simplistic theories of the past were right in some instances and wrong in others. Lowie's encyclopedic knowledge was such that his critics could not really dispute him; the best they could do was to accuse him of intellectual anarchism. The quintessential Lowie was revealed in the last paragraph of *Primitive Culture:* "To that planless hodge-podge, that thing of shreds and patches called civilization [i.e. culture], the historian can no longer yield superstitious reverence. He will understand better than others the obstacles to infusing design into the amorphous product . . . ." (Lowie 1920, 441). (In a later edition Lowie sought to distance himself from this statement, but his alibi was not very convincing; see Lowie 1950, ix-x).

What was true of culture in general was true in particular of kinship studies, Lowie's area of special interest. The early theorists had without exception sought to expand their ideas on kinship into general evolutionary schemes, which were the "rage of the age." These became the special target of much of Lowie's criticism. Together with a number of fellow Boasian ethnographers, he successfully dealt a death blow to imagined evolutionary schemes in general, and to those related to kinship in particular, by burying them under masses of contrary data. And without its evolutionary component, kinship theory lost much of its cogency. At all events, the heat was gone. Lowie did not by any means end the kinship discourse, but he did for all practical purposes end the wars. No one again got nearly so angry as McLennan, Lang, and Kohler.

CHAPTER SEVENTEEN

RETROSPECT

Speculation about the origin and the earliest development of human society can be traced back at least to early Greek times (Adams 1998, 12-16). It became moot for a time in the middle ages, when Biblical tradition was accepted as a sufficient answer, but was revived by the secularist philosophers of the Enlightenment. Then, with the discovery of the true antiquity of man in the middle of the nineteenth century, the field for speculation was vastly enlarged, and it became one of the truly exciting topics for the European and American intelligentsia of the Victorian age. Out of their speculations arose, in time, the discipline of anthropology as we understand it.

Early on, two rather distinct schools of thought about early human society developed. The theory-driven sociological school, which flourished in Britain and America, had its roots in the Scottish Enlightenment. Avowedly progressivist, its adherents spun out sweeping, relatively simple schemes of social evolution envisioned as a course of continual progress; schemes that rested heavily on logic. The data-driven ethnological school, flourishing in Germanic countries and inspired by the particularist philosophy of Immanuel Kant, looked for guidance rather to the most primitive societies that could be identified in the present or the recent past. The two schools were not wholly distinct; the British and American theorists cited ethnographic evidence to the extent that it supported their preconceived theories, while the Germanics at times had no choice but to fall back on logic.

The kinship wars were an important though ambiguous byproduct of this larger discourse. Everyone agreed that kinship was critically important, because it was so much more elaborately developed in primitive than in modern societies. At the same time, opinions differed widely as to how to fit it into the evolutionary scheme. In any case, the distinct roles of the sociological and the ethnographic schools are quite clearly recognizable throughout the debate. The British and Americans from Maine to Hartland spun out lofty general schemes, while the Germanics from Starcke to Lowie continually pointed out that things were not that simple. In the end it was the Germanic perspective that won out, thanks to the fieldwork revolution at the beginning of the twentieth century. The simplistic theories of the armchair scholars simply could not sustain the weight of ethnographic evidence

In the twentieth century, social anthropologists both in Britain and in America tired of the debate, for which there could be no final solution, and they largely turned their backs on evolutionary speculation. Most Americans at the same time turned their backs on kinship studies; they survived as the province only of a small, specialized group of enthusiasts. There was some revival of interest in evolutionary theory beginning in the 1960s, but it rested on material, not on social evidence

It was different for the British, for they still had one more "discovery" to make. Working mainly in Africa, in the era between the first and second World Wars, they discovered segmentary lineage systems. Tribes with neither chiefs nor overt stratification were found to regulate themselves through a sense of common ancestry that extended through the whole tribe (see especially Radcliffe-Brown and Forde 1950; Middleton and Tait 1958). Thus, kinship continued to provide the basis for understanding everything about their society and polity. Adam Kuper (1973) was later to argue that his colleagues had vastly exaggerated this organizing principle, and had "found" segmentary lineage systems where none actually existed. However, for a generation they dominated British social theory as totemism had once dominated religious theory.

In sum, the kinship wars were a byproduct of the Victorians' preoccupation with social evolution, as that in turn was a reflection of their boundless faith in progress. The mindless cataclysm of World War I, from 1914 to 1918, dealt a nearly fatal blow to all of them.

CHAPTER EIGHTEEN

THE LEGACY

Of all the grand theories of the kinship warriors, the only one that has fully stood the test of time is Maine's conception of the evolution of society from status to contract. Yet for all that, anthropology owes a lasting debt to all the warriors, not for their theories but for their concepts. With matriliny, exogamy, polyandry, totemism, sororate, levirate, avunculate, teknonymy, and a host of other terms they have given us nearly the whole of the technical vocabulary that makes discussion of the subject possible. And, as Lowie (1937, 281) long ago observed, "Clarification of concepts . . . directly gauges scientific progress." Theories come and go, but concepts endure. They are the true foundation blocks of human understanding.

GLOSSARY OF KINSHIP AND
OTHER RELATIONAL TERMS

Achieved status. A recognized social position acquired by an individual in the course of his or her lifetime; not inherited at birth. Educational degrees, military ranks, and in-law relationships are all examples of achieved status.

Affines; affinal kinship. All persons related to an individual through his or her spouse; in-laws as they would be called in ordinary parlance.

Agnates; agnatic kinship. Persons related to an individual through the father. The term originated in Roman law.

Agnation. See *Patrilineal descent.*

Ascribed status. A recognized social position ascribed to an individual more or less automatically, without any action on his or her part. It is usually though not always conferred at birth. Gender identity as well as membership in a lineage, a clan, or a religious sect are examples of ascribed status.

Avunculate. A social system, usually *matrilineal*, in which the mother's brother stands in a specially close relationship to a person.

Bilateral kinship. A social system in which social status, rights and obligations may be inherited from either the father or the mother, or both.

Bride capture. A marital practice, in *exogamous* societies, in which a bride must be captured by force from a kin group other than one's own. Although often imagined, and mentioned in mythology, there are no known examples of this practice among living peoples.

Clan. For anthropologists, a large, widely dispersed kin group composed of individuals who claim descent from a common ancestor far back in time, and who therefore may be known by a common clan name, but who cannot verify their membership by reciting an actual genealogy. Because of the belief in a kinship bond, clans are usually *exogamous,* and may be either *matrilineal* or *patrilineal.* Unlike the *lineage,* however, the clan does not have a specific territory of its own, or a political leader. Clans, as the term is used by anthropologists, are mostly found in tribal societies. They are not to be confused with the Scottish clan, which is *endogamous* and has a distinct territory and a political leader. Because of possible confusion with the Scottish clan, some anthropologists prefer the term *sib* for dispersed, non-territorial clans found among tribal peoples.

Cognates; cognatic kin. Persons related to an individual through the mother. The term originated in Roman law.

Consanguinal kin. Persons related by blood, or in other words descended from a common ancestor at some point in the past, as distinguished from relatives by marriage (*affinal kin*).

Corporate kin group. A group of closely related individuals who own their land, animals, and other productive resources in common, and share together in the labor and the rewards deriving therefrom. Normally, though not always, the members of a corporate kin group live close together. This is the common socio-economic system found in most tribal societies, and was also present among the Greeks, Romans, and other ancient peoples.

Culturology; cultural determinism. The belief, common to most American anthropologists today, that people's thoughts and actions are determined primarily by their culture.

Endogamy. A marital system in which individuals should marry someone from within their own group. In the case of kin groups this is rarely an absolutely rigid rule, since there may not by any suitable mates available. It is more commonly applied rigorously in the case of religious groups.

Exogamy. A marital system in which a person must marry someone from outside his or her own kin group. It derives from the abhorrence of incest that seems to be common in all human societies. However, definitions of incest vary widely as to what categories of kin are and are not included. In modern western society, the only exogamous group is the nuclear family, composed of parents, brothers and sisters. In many other societies, however, more distant kin including cousins, uncles and aunts, and others may also be forbidden as mates. In societies having clans, the whole clan is normally an exogamous unit; one must marry from another clan. Unlike the case of *endogamy*, exogamous rules are nearly always rigid, not preferential.

Extended family, extended kin group. A group of related individuals, larger than the *nuclear family*, who feel a strong sense of family and who interact with one another at least intermittently. In addition to the nuclear family it regularly includes various kinds of aunts, uncles and cousins. The group may or may not be *corporate* in the strict sense, but the members will normally cooperate in circumstances where a lot of individuals are needed—perhaps most often in putting on weddings and funerals.

Fictive kinship. A concept under which individuals are formally and legally attached to a kin group, even though they do not belong by birth. The adoption of children into a family is the primary example of fictive kinship found in modern society, but there are many other categories of fictive kin in simpler societies.

Group marriage. An imagined state in which a group of men is collectively married to a group of women, with sexual rights freely shared among them. Early anthropological theorists, who viewed the first human societies as highly promiscuous, often imagined them as practicing group marriage. But although temporary sharing of spouses within a group is fairly common, a true, permanent state of group marriage has never been recorded among living peoples except in certain eccentric religious groups.

Horde. A large group of individuals (or animals) living in proximity and regularly interacting with one another, but having no organization or leadership. Although common among animals, no such grouping has actually been found among humans.

Kinship nomenclature. The system of terms by which different kinds of kin (parents, uncles, aunts, grandparents, *affinal kin* and the like) are designated in a particular society. The systems are quite variable; for example, it is common for uncles and aunts to be designated by the same terms as parents, and for cousins to be designated the same as siblings. Among all peoples, seven recurring systems of kinship nomenclature have been recognized, along with numerous variants.

Levirate. A legal principle holding that when a man dies, his brothers inherit responsibility for the support of his widow or widows, and consequently marry them.

Lineage. A very *extended kin group;* that is, an extended group of individuals who are descended from a common ancestor, and can verify it by means of a genealogy. Membership may be inherited either through the mother *(matrilineal)* or the father *(patrilineal)*. Unlike the *clan,* the lineage is very often a *corporate group* and will often have a recognized territory and a formal leader.

Matriarchy. A political system in which supreme authority is exercised by females, and is normally inherited from mothers to daughters. While modern nations are sometimes ruled by a queen, as were some ancient ones, their authority has always been inherited from a father or husband, within what is normally a patriarchal system. They are in effect substitute men, and are treated as such. At the level of the nation or tribe there has never been a truly matriarchal society, although matriarchy may prevail in certain kin and religious groups.

Matrilineal descent, matriliny. A socioeconomic system in which social status, property, and a variety of rights and obligations are inherited from the mother, by both males and females. Matrilineal societies are found mainly among tribal peoples, although by no means all tribes are matrilineal. It was once believed that all the earliest human societies were matrilineal, because of uncertainty about paternity, but this view is now almost universally discredited. None of the most primitive societies known today are matrilineal.

The problem of what factors lead to the development of matrilineal kinship reckoning continues to be debated among anthropologists.

Matrilocal residence. A socioeconomic rule under which a newly married couple goes to live with or near the family of the bride, and becomes a part of her *extended kin group,* sharing in the labor and resources of the group. In practice it goes most often hand in hand with matrilineal society, though this is not universally the case. In any case it is necessarily a preference rather than a rigid rule; there may always be practical reasons why newlyweds should live with the husband's group (*patrilocal residence)* or by themselves *neolocal residence).* The term is slightly misleading since *matri-,* speaking literally, refers to the mother rather than the wife; for this reason some anthropologists prefer the term *uxorilocal residence.*

Moiety. When a society is divided into two counter-balancing halves, they are termed moieties. They are usually though not always very widely extended kin groups, in which the members of each consider themselves descendants of a common ancestor. They are found chiefly in tribal societies. Very commonly they alternate in holding political or religious authority in the course of the year.

Monandry. A social system in which a woman is permitted no more than one husband. It is the opposite of *polyandry.*

Neolocal residence. A social system in which a married couple finds its own place to live, apart from both the husband's and the wife's family. It has become usual in modern times, particularly in America, but was decidedly rare earlier.

Nuclear family. The minimum kin group, consisting of a couple and their children, that exists in nearly all societies. It is nearly always resident under a common roof, but has no other universal defining characteristics. In America and most other western countries it is the only property-owning and co-dependent kin group recognized under law, but in many other societies it is embedded in a more *extended kin group* with whom it shares property, rights and obligations.

Patria potestas. A legal concept under which a man is granted absolute and unlimited power over his wife and children, and sometimes more extended kin as well.

Patriarchy. A social system in which all authority as exercised by males.

Patrilineal descent, patriliny. A socioeconomic system in which social status, property, and a variety of rights and obligations are inherited from the father, by both males and females. This is the system of descent and inheritance reckoning found in virtually all complex societies, but also in many simpler ones.

Patrilocal residence. A socioeconomic rule under which a newly married couple goes to live with or near the family of the husband, and becomes a part of his *extended kin group,* sharing in the labor and resources of the group. In Western society this was the normal residence rule in medieval and all earlier times, although today it has been largely supplanted by the rule of *neolocal residence.*

Polyandry. A social system in which a woman may have more than one husband. It is and has always been highly uncommon.

Polygamy. A social system in which a man may have more than one wife (*polygyny*) or a woman may have more than one husband (*polyandry*).

Polygyny. A social system in which a man may have more than one wife. Outside the Christian world it is very common, particularly where circumstances have produced a shortage of males. It is never of course universal or prescribed; having more than one wife is commonly regarded as a sign of wealth.

Sib. See *Clan.*

Sodality. A formally organized and self-recognizing group of individuals who are drawn together by common interests or circumstances other than kinship. Clubs of one kind or another, existing in may societies, are examples of sodalities.

Sororate. A legal principle under which, if a woman dies, her husband is entitled to one of her sisters as a substitute, without payment of additional bride fees.

Totemism, totem. The belief by members of an extended kin group that they are all descended from a common supernatural ancestor—

most often conceived as an animal but sometimes also as a plant. The mythical ancestor (*totem*) becomes an object of veneration and special ceremonies for the group.

Unilineal systems. Social systems in which descent and inheritance are reckoned exclusively through the father (*patrilineal*) or exclusively through the mother (*matrilineal*).

Uxorilocal residence. See *Matrilocal residence*.

Virilocal residence. See *Patrilocal residence*.

BIBLIOGRAPHY

Adams, William Y. *Shonto: a Study of the Role of the Trader in a Modern Navaho Community. Bureau of American Ethnology Bulletin* 188, 1963.

----------. *The Philosophical Roots of Anthropology.* Stanford, 1998.

----------. *Religion and Adaptation.* Stanford, 2005.

Armstrong, William H. *Warrior in Two Camps.* Syracuse, 1978.

Bachofen, Johann J. *Das Mutterrecht: seine Untrusting uber die Gynaekokratie der alten Welt nach hirer religiösen und rechlichen Natur.* Stuttgart, 1861.

----------. *Myth, Religion, and Mother Right; Selected Writings of J. J. Bachofen*, translated from the German by Ralph Manheim. London, 1967.

Barnes, R. H. "Editor's Introduction, in Kohler" 1975, 1-70.

Burridge, Kenelm. *Encountering Aborigines.* New York, 1973.

Crawley, Ernest. *The Mystic Rose.* London, 1902.

----------. *The Mystic Rose,* revised and enlarged by Theodore Besterman. London, 1927

Daniel, Glyn. *The Idea of Prehistory.* Harmondsworth, 1950.

Durkheim, Émile. *Les Formes Élementaires de la Vie Religieuse.* Paris, 1912.

Elliot Smith, G. "Preface," in Rivers 1926.

Evans-Pritchard, E. E. *A History of Anthropological Thought.* New York, 1981.

Frazer, James G. *Totemism and Exogamy* (4 vols.). London, 1910.

Freud, Sigmund. *Totem and Tabu.* London, 1913.

Goldenweiser, Alexander.. "Totemism, an Analytical Study." *Journal of American Folklore* 23, 179-294. 1910.

Grant Duff, M. E. *Sir Henry Maine; a Brief Memoir of his Life.* New York, 1892.

Hartland, William Sidney. *Primitive Paternity: the Myth of Supernatural Birth in Relation to the Family* (2 vols.). London, 1909-10.

----------. *Matrilineal Kinship and the Question of its Priority. American Anthropological Association Memoir* 4, 1917.

----------. *Primitive Society.* London, 1921.

Kardiner, Abram, and Edward Preble. *They Studied Man.* Cleveland, 1961.

Kohler, Josef. *Zur Urgeschichte der Ehe.* Stuttgart, 1897.

----------. *Philosophy of Law.* New York, 1921.

----------. *On the Prehistory of Marriage,* translated from the German by R. H. Barnes and Ruth Barnes; edited and with an introduction by R. H. Barnes. Chicago, 1975

Kuper, Adam. *Anthropologists and Anthropology, the British School 1922-1972.* London, 1973.

Lafitau, Joseph. *Customs of the American Indians Compared with the Customs of Earliest Times,* translated and edited by William N. Fenton and Elizabeth L. Moore. Toronto. 1974 (French original 1724).

Lang, Andrew. *Custom and Myth.* London, 1884.

----------. *Myth, Religion and Ritual* (2 vols.). London, 1887.

----------. *The Making of Religion.* London, 1898.

----------. *Social Origins.* London, 1903.

----------. *The Secret of the Totem.* London, 1905.

Lee, Richard, and Irven Devore, eds. *Man the Hunter.* Chicago, 1968.

Locke, John. *Two Treatises on Government.* London, 1690.

Lonergan, David. "Lang, Andrew," in Winters 1991, 379-80.

Lowie, Robert H. *Primitive Society.* New York, 1920.

----------. *The Origin of the State.* New York, 1927.

----------. *The Crow Indians.* New York, 1935.

----------. (ed.). *Essays in Anthropology Presented to A. L. Kroeber.* Berkeley, 1936.

----------. *The History of Ethnological Theory*. New York, 1937.

----------. *Primitive Culture, Black and Gold Edition*. New York, 1947.

----------. *Social Organization*. New York, 1948.

----------. *Robert H. Lowie, Ethnologist*. Berkeley, 1959.

Maine, Henry Sumner. *Ancient Law*. London, 1861.

----------. *Lectures on the Early History of Institutions*. London, 1875.

----------. *Dissertations on Early Law and Customs*. London, 1883.

----------. *Ancient Law*, 10th Edition. London, 1884.

----------. *Ancient Law*, 10th Edition, with Introduction and Notes by Sir Frederick Pollock. New York, 1920.

McLennan, John F. *Primitive Marriage*. Edinburgh, 1865.

----------. *Studies in Ancient History Comprising a Reprint of Primitive Marriage*. London, 1876.

----------. *The Patriarchal Theory*, edited and completed by Donald McLennan. London, 1885.

----------. *Primitive Marriage*, edited and with an Introduction by Peter Rivière. Chicago, 1970

Middleton, John, and David Tait, eds. *Tribes without Rulers*. London, 1958.

Morgan, Lewis Henry. *League of the Ho-dé-no-sau-nee or Iroquois*. Rochester, 1851.

----------. *The American Beaver and His Works*. Philadelphia, 1868.

----------. *Systems of Consanguinity and Affinity of the Human Family*. Washington: *Smithsonian Contributions to Knowledge* 218, 1871.

----------. "Montezuma's Dinner," *North American Review* 122, 265-308, 1876.

----------. *Ancient Society*. New York, 1877.

----------. *Houses and House-life of the American Aborigines*. Washington, 1881.

Mucke, Johann Richard. *Horde und Familie in ihrer urgeshichtlichen Entwicklung: Eine neue Theorie auf statistlicher Grundlage*. Stuttgart, 1895.

Murphy, Robert F. *Robert H. Lowie*. New York, 1972.

Needham, Rodney. "Editor's Introduction," in Wake 1967.

Oppenheimer, Fritz. *Der Staat*. Leipzig, 1907

Piaget, Jean. *The Child's Conception of the World,* trans. J. and A. Tomlinson. Totowa, 1960.

Pollock, Frederick. "Introduction," in Maine 1920, xiii-xxiv.

Radcliffe-Brown, A. R.. "The Study of Kinship Systems," *Journal of the Royal Anthropological Institute* 71, 1-18, 1941.

----------., and Daryll Forde, eds.. *African Systems of Kinship and Marriage.* London, 1950.

Radin, Paul. *Primitive Religion.* New York, 1937.

Resek, Carl. *Lewis Henry Morgan: American Scholar.* Chicago, 1960.

Rivers, W. H. R.. *The Todas.* London, 1906.

----------. *The History of Melanesian Society* (2 vols.) Cambridge, 1914a.

----------. *Kinship and Social Organization.* London, 1914b.

----------. *Social Organization.* London, 1920.

----------. *Conflicts and Dreams.* London, 1923.

----------. *Social Organization,* Second Impression (Revised), edited by W. J. Perry. London, 1926.

Rivière, Peter. "Introduction," in McLennan 1970.

Smith, W. Robertson. *Kinship and Marriage in Early Arabia.* Cambridge, 1885.

----------. *Lectures on the Religion of the Semites.* London, 1889.

Spier, Leslie. "The Distribution of Kinship Systems in North America," *University of Washington Publications in Anthropology* 1, 69-88, 1925.

Starcke, C. N.. *Die primitive Familie und ihrer Entstehung und Entwicklung.* Leipzig, 1888,

----------. *The Primitive Family in its Origin and Development.* New York, 1894.

Steward, Julian. "The Economic and Social Basis of Primitive Bands," in Lowie 1936, 331-45. 1936.

----------. *Theory of Culture Change.* Urbana 1955.

Tylor, E. B. *Anahuac.* London, 1861.

----------. *Researches into the Early History of Mankind.* London, 1865.

----------. *Primitive Culture* (2 vols.). London, 1871.

----------. *Anthropology.* London, 1881.

----------. "On a Method of Investigating the Development of Institutions Applied to Laws of Marriage and Descent," *Journal of the Royal Anthropological Institute* 18, 245-69. 1889.

Wake, C. Staniland. *The Evolution of Morality, Being a History of the Development of Moral Culture* (2 vols.). London, 1878.

----------. *The Development of Marriage and Kinship.* London, 1889.

----------. *The Development of Marriage and Kinship,* edited and with an Introduction by Rodney Needham. Chicago, 1967.

Westermarck, Edward. *The History of Human Marriage.* London, 1891.

----------. *The Origin and Development of the Moral Ideas* (2 vols.). London, 1906-8.

----------. *The History of Human Marriage,* 5th ed. (3 vols.). London. 1921.

----------. *Ritual and Belief in Morocco* (2 vols.) London, 1926a.

----------. *A Short History of Marriage.* London, 1926b.

----------. *Wit and Wisdom in Morocco.* London, 1930.

Winters, Christopher, ed., *International Dictionary of Anthropologists.* New York, 1991.

www.ingramcontent.com/pod-product-compliance
Lightning Source LLC
Chambersburg PA
CBHW050402290526
45786CB00003B/1098